F. Scott Fitzgerald's

The Great Gatsby:

BOOKMARKED

JAIME CLARKE

Kirby Gann, *Series Editor*

PUBLISHING

NEW YORK

Ig Publishing
Box 2547
New York, NY 10163
www.igpub.com

ISBN: 978-1-63246-039-4 (paperback)

PRINTED IN THE UNITED STATES OF AMERICA
FIRST EDITION | FIRST PRINTING

For Mary

James Gatz

Sometime in the middle of my sophomore year in high school, my old grade-school friend casually mentioned that I should attend classes with him for a day at Brophy College Preparatory, the private all-boys Catholic school he attended rather than enrolling at Tolleson Union High School, the public school the rest of us had migrated to, such shadowing being encouraged by Brophy, which was always looking to expand its student body. My old grade-school friend tantalized me with the long list of holidays Brophy students enjoyed—not just the state and federal holidays, but religious holidays as well—and even though I doubted my family could afford the tuition, Brophy's elite reputation compelled me to say yes, so I agreed, registering to be a shadow for a day.

The first thing I noticed about Brophy was that its parking lot resembled a dealership lot, one specializing in foreign cars. Where the vehicles at Tolleson gave the distinct impression that the current owners were not the original owners, the BMWs, Mercedeses, and Volkswagens populating the Brophy parking lot were shiny and new, their seamless paint jobs sparkling in the sunlight. My old grade-school friend pulled his pearl BMW 323i into the sophomore parking lot, and I followed him through his schedule of classes, easily blending in with the other boys, mostly white, all with collared shirts and haircuts short enough not to touch the collar. We lunched in the courtyard, sitting around the fountain munching slices of pizza from Appetito's, an outlet of the chain restaurant that stood in for any kind of cafeteria. I marveled at the Spanish colonial architecture, especially the bell tower situated atop Regis Hall, the administration building. My old grade-school friend pointed out the students with surnames I recognized from the newspaper: a congressman's youngest son, a famous golfer's son, the son of Phoenix's richest business-man. Enamored as I was with Brophy, though, I felt certain that it was a brass ring too high. In fact, my old grade-school friend's appearances at Tolleson's parties over the years had yielded the impression that friends at Brophy were hard to come by, and I guessed that if you hadn't gone to any of the elementary schools in the exclusive communities with names like Paradise Valley and Scottsdale that fed the student population, you were perennially on the outside looking in. I kept my concerns to myself, though, and went forward with the application, curious to know if I would be accepted, if only on paper.

I'd mostly forgotten about the application by the time my acceptance arrived, coming as it did at a crucial point in my academic career. As my sophomore year at Tolleson wound down, it became abundantly clear that my friendships with upperclassmen had unintentionally alienated me from my peers. I realized that my true friends would be graduating at the end of the school year, leaving me behind, a stranger among my classmates. This more than anything fueled my decision to accept my admittance to Brophy, working out the financial arrangements with my parents after the fact. I knew if need be, I could contribute something with the money I made serving greasy food at Pete's Fish & Chips, the beloved fast-food establishment in Tolleson, a block from my former high school. My old grade-school friend's father was the manager, and we'd begged him to hire us the summer before high school so we could earn money to finance our teenage years. I kept my impending transfer a secret until the last week of my sophomore year, and I realized a little wistfully that Yearbook Day was my last day at Tolleson.

Daisy

I'd failed to mention my shadow day at Brophy, or my application, or my acceptance, to Jenny, who heard about it from someone else during that last week. She thought it was a joke, and I realized that I purposely hadn't told her, that I'd cheated on our relationship by keeping it a secret, mostly out of cowardice. The hurt on her face made me regret the entire episode, and even though later in life I'd swear to any who asked that it was a mistake to transfer from public school to private, I knew the momentum of my switching schools—or rather the impulse to transfer to Brophy—would carry me farther than just the Brophy campus. I had no way of knowing, though, that it was the beginning of the end of us, or that the good-bye would be so painful, the aftermath haunting me for years.

Sophomore year I had met and fallen in love with Jenny, a freshman saxophone player in my section. I was drawn to her immediately; our senses of humor were in sync, but I also recognized that while she could be as sarcastic and ironic as the rest of us, there was an earnestness about her that wouldn't ever be forsaken. It seemed she possessed an inner strength that others believed I possessed, but I knew that I did not, and I often felt as helpless as a flag rent in the wind.

"She's a Mormon, dude," someone said when I confirmed my interest.

I shrugged, unsure of what that meant.

I quickly assimilated into Jenny's circle of friends, which I learned were mostly Mormon. The Mormon kids on campus were not a small population and were generally good students and well regarded, an association I liked to think enhanced my reputation. Jenny, too, was Mormon, her family being a first-generation conversion (someone her father worked with had convinced them to convert), and when, upon meeting me, her mother asked her in front of me if I was LDS, I was oblivious to her mother's meaning. Jenny answered that I wasn't, and I let the matter drop, my happiness at being with Jenny blocking out the white noise around us. My long hours at Pete's were not a source of frustration to our fledgling love, as her parents wouldn't allow us to date officially until Jenny turned sixteen, so our courtship took place entirely at school or at her house after school, before my work shift started.

Still, the ease and speed with which our relationship grew serious might've been alarming to Jenny's parents, but their recent separation consumed them, and Jenny and I were mostly left alone, free to wander her family's property outside of Tolleson, a parcel among parcels in what was primarily unused farmland. We rode the family three-wheeler back and forth to her cousin's house, at the other end of the farmland; sometimes we took her horse, who spooked me. Mostly we watched television or listened to music while we shot pool in her living room, her billiard skills far superior to mine.

Sometimes I listened to her practice the violin for her performances with the Phoenix Symphony Youth Orchestra, the sound of the violin transporting me. I was always aware that her mother was lurking around the house, though, maybe looking out a window or listening for the quiet that portends making out. Jenny's home was a sanctuary that offered us a place out of time in which to get to know each other. That she had never seen my house (her mother forbade her to go to my house alone) or met my family, or that we didn't hang out with my friends and their girlfriends, was not a concern and in fact nicely complemented my busy school and work schedule. Because of her parents' restrictions, our only socializing as a couple was attending Mormon dances. Every so often a couple of Mormon stakes (each church or ward was part of a stake; Jenny belonged to the Garden Lakes ward, which in turn belonged to the West Maricopa stake) got together and hosted a dance.

Anyone could participate in the dances, regardless of religion; however, before attending your first dance, you had to acquire a dance card from the local bishop. I made the requisite appointment, swinging by the ward before reporting to work at Pete's. The bishop, an older man undifferentiated from the other church elders, welcomed me and asked me into his spartan office. We exchanged a few pleasantries—I told him about how Jenny was my girlfriend and ran down the roster of my friends who attended the Garden Lakes ward—and then settled into business. The bishop handed me a small yellow piece of paper, the dance card I'd come for, invalid without the bishop's signature, which he was happy to provide after I read and consented to the rules on the back of the card:

1. Ages 14–18
2. Valid dance card must be presented at the door for admission. (We will accept valid dance cards from other stakes.) Replacement charge for lost card is $5.00.
3. The Word of Wisdom is to be observed: No tobacco, alcohol, or drugs are permitted inside the building or on the premises.
4. BOYS shall wear dress pants (no Levi's, jeans, denims, or imitations of any color, or other non–dress pants). Shirts must have collars. No sandals are allowed. (Nice tennis shoes are OK.) Socks must be worn with shoes. No hats, earrings, or gloves.
5. GIRLS shall not wear tight-fitting dresses or skirts or have bare shoulders (blouses and dresses must have sleeves). Hemlines of dresses are to be of modest length (to the knee). No dresses or skirts with slits or cuts above the knee.
6. After admittance to the dance, you are to remain inside the building.
7. No loitering or sitting in cars on church grounds.
8. Automobiles shall be driven in a quiet and courteous manner, so as not to disturb the residents in the area.
9. No acrobatics, bear-hugging, bumping, rolling on floor, or exhibitions.
10. Personal conduct and behavior shall be that expected from exemplary young ladies and gentlemen.

"Can you agree to these rules?" the bishop asked.

I said that I could.

"Very good," he said, taking the slip of paper from me and ceremoniously signing his name to it. "Have you considered joining our church?" he asked as he handed me what I'd come for.

I hadn't. "I might," I said, knowing that was the answer he wanted to hear. He regarded me cautiously.

"You might attend with Jenny and her family," the bishop said. I wondered if he knew about Jenny's parents' marital status, guessing that he didn't. The topic was never broached in Jenny's house, or in her cousin's house, everyone pretending like the fact that Jenny's mother and father were still married but not living in the same house was unremarkable.

"I work on Sundays, is the thing," I explained.

"Ah," the bishop said. "No rest for the wicked, eh?" I couldn't tell if the bishop was joking or not, so I laughed, suppressing a sickening feeling that was building in my stomach. The next question caught me off guard. "Have you and Jenny been intimate?"

I answered no automatically, not just because it was the truth, but because I hoped the answer would stifle the look of surprise on my face.

"Have you been tempted?" he asked.

I fumbled through a series of "ums" and "wells," stuttering until I gave up and smiled.

"It's okay," the bishop said. "We're all tempted. Moral character is defined by how we react to temptation. I hope you'll continue to consider your moral character in the face of temptation. And Jenny's, too."

I assured him I would, and we both stood, shaking hands.

An Oxford Man

My enrollment at Brophy for my junior year was like starting high school all over again. I realized during the first week of classes at Brophy that I would not be able to move freely between the different cliques and social groups, as I had at Tolleson, for the simple reason that the social stratosphere at Brophy was divided into two castes: those whose families had money and those who didn't. The realization did not burden me with bitterness; instead I whiled away my spare moments contemplating a burgeoning fascination with wealth. I wondered what it was like not to have to work or be responsible for monthly bills. I wondered if my classmates had access to allowances, or if they had to negotiate every time they wanted money. I wondered if having money meant you didn't notice how some things were expensive and some things weren't, each expenditure separate from the next, rather than having a cumulative effect, as it was for people without unlimited means.

These questions coincided with the study of *The Great Gatsby*, by F. Scott Fitzgerald, in Mr. H——'s American lit class. Mr. H—— was a youngish man who liked to tell the story of how he met his wife, a stockbroker. ("I went in look-ing for a stock, came out with a bond.") He had written a sub-stantial paper on *The Great Gatsby* in college and even brought it into class as a prop. Jay Gatsby and his self-invention for the direct purpose of impressing and winning back Daisy Buchanan, the rich girl who married the equally rich Tom Buchanan rather than wait for the poor James Gatz to trans-form into Jay Gatsby—and the singularity of purpose Gatsby held fast to in order to realize his goal—occupied my daily thoughts. I had no inkling the novel would haunt me not just in the near future, but also for decades after, that it would mir-ror my life so closely.

I marveled at how F. Scott Fitzgerald had written some-thing that people were reading long after he had died. In the fifth grade, I'd bragged to my teacher, Miss Kephart, that I'd read all the Hardy Boys books and that I could probably write one. She challenged me to do just that, offering to type up my handwritten pages and to schedule weekly editorial meetings. I had no intention of writing the book, to be sure, but when Miss Kephart asked me about it again later in the week, I sensed her desire to participate in the project. And her desire fed my desire to impress her. I was a new kid at the start of the fifth grade—my third elementary school in as many years—and I'd learned the value of currying favor with teachers. If writing a book was something adults respected, then I would endeavor to write one. I agreed to the proposal, handing in my scribbled pages at our meetings, Wednesdays after school, Miss Kephart going over the typed version of my offerings from the week before, pointing out redundancies, encourag-ing me to vary my language. By the end of the school year, *The*

Mystery of Dead Man's Grave was complete, ready to go out to publishers, all of whom rejected the manuscript. My interest in the project dissipated before all the rejections had boomeranged back from New York in the envelopes with postage that I'd provided. Now a junior, I hadn't thought about writing since and didn't associate my fifth-grade project with what Fitzgerald and writers like him had accomplished. That anyone regardless of background could create something that would pass from generation to generation was too thrilling to be believed, and I knew with certainty I wanted to be immortal in that way, or at least to try.

•

As my classmates tried to parse the meaning of the green light at the end of Daisy's dock, or the vivid imagery of the valley of ashes, I silently identified with the nomadic upbringing the young James Gatz endured on his way to becoming Jay Gatsby. My recent move from public school to private was just another maneuver in a chain that had begun when my family left my hometown in Montana for the Dakotas, first North and then South. Phoenix was like moving to Mars, comparatively, but it was also just another move. I no longer considered myself from Montana, never did feel Dakotan and struggled to identify as a Phoenician, as most of the city's residents were retirees from somewhere else. I had been the new kid in class so many times over that I embraced my status as an exotic bird. Like Gatsby, I was an immigrant in my native land, and

I marveled for the first time at how that might be considered an attribute rather than the bummer it seemed.

•

But I was both inside Fitzgerald's pages and out: The immediate effect of my reading (and rereading) *The Great Gatsby* was an inspiration to become wealthy like Gatsby. Part of my reinvention as a Brophy Bronco involved a hastily conceived fitness regimen featuring late-night/early-morning weekend jogs up and down Camelback Mountain on the east side of Phoenix. At a peak elevation of thirteen hundred feet, Camelback barely qualified as a mountain, but its dromedaric features could be seen from almost anywhere on the valley floor, and the population of multimillion-dollar homes up and down the camel's back gave it an air of awe and mystery, not to mention the privacy it afforded teenagers who were looking for a quiet place to park.

My old grade-school friend and I began jogging the streets after our shifts at Pete's ended, sometime near midnight, huffing and panting as we raced each other through the clean, paved streets. I began to know the order of the houses and wondered what kinds of lives were lived behind the doors and windows of the luxury homes that hardly looked lived in. I imagined myself strolling out a patio door of the house with an unobstructed view of the Phoenix skyline, a cocktail in hand, my hair slick from an earlier swim. Or wandering out onto the balcony of the Spanish castle built into the south side of the mountain. Or I imagined myself playing tennis on the court you could glimpse through a stand of well-maintained oleanders. I couldn't readily imagine what kind of job allowed someone to have a house like those on Camelback Mountain, and when, upon the start of the school year, I learned that most of the fathers of my classmates were lawyers, I struck up a fascination with the law, determined to become a high-powered attorney.

On one particular late-night jog, a three-tiered house I was especially enthralled with had sprouted a for sale sign. It was the sort of immense house that Gatsby would've aspired to. I was just as quickly disappointed, however, when closer inspection of the sign revealed that showings were "by appointment only." The inside of the mansion would remain a mystery after all, I supposed, the for sale sign mocking me as I jogged past it week after week. Then, one lucky day, the sign was amended with information about an open house that Saturday. I realized my luck and quickly set about concocting a plan that would plausibly explain why a teenager was attending the open house solo. I considered dressing up as a mailman but had no way to secure a USPS regulation uniform before the weekend. I wondered if a brown shirt and a brown pair of pants would be enough to fool the real estate agents into thinking I was with UPS. I could tuck an empty box wrapped in brown paper under my arm, then realize that I'd delivered to the wrong house only as the real estate agents pointed out the address on the box, written in my own hand. The absence of a UPS truck would be a dead giveaway, I reasoned.

Finally I lit upon the right scheme, one I was sure no adult could argue against. I would simply say that I was a student at

Brophy and was working on a class project that involved my videotaping various architectural structures. I would be purposefully vague if pressed on the nature of the project, peppering my answers with phrases like "still in the early stages" and "shooting a lot of raw footage," etc. I had only to borrow a video camera; my old grade-school friend lent me his without his parents' knowing.

Gaining access to the mansion was alarmingly easy, though I guessed that it had less to do with my cover story than with the fact that I interrupted the two real estate agents in charge of showing the property from whatever they were doing in the mirrored weight room. The agents looked me over and answered my question about the outlets having power for my video camera, then disappeared somewhere in the house; the woman's lilting laughter would later be heard in the background of the videotape.

I stalked through each floor of the empty house, panning to catch the enormous bedrooms, the elevator between floors, the surprisingly small kitchen, and the living room, slowly pointing the camera out the window, over the infinity pool, and off into the distance to capture the Phoenix skyline. The house was devoid of prospective buyers, and I let my imagination wander, fantasizing about bounding through the front door after a hard day of Conquering the World, greeting my wife, going for a dip to cleanse the day's troubles, cooling off with cocktails, and relaxing on an expensive leather couch, staring into the gloaming as the sun settled over the city. I pictured my imaginary self as I waltzed through the house, drunk with the world of wealth, an inebriation that led to further investigation: I put my name and address on the lists for catalogs from high-end clothing stores like Ralph Lauren, as well as The Sharper Image, whose extraordinarily expensive gadgetry bespoke a lifestyle of white linen suits and green lawns.

I searched for how I could start the metamorphosis from lowly fast-food worker to the stratosphere of the wealthy elite. My first order of business was to get a better car. I traded in my midnight-blue Wolfsburg Edition Volkswagen Rabbit with personalized plates reading MY HARE for a red Nissan Pulsar NX with personalized plates that read O2B YNG, complete with removable T-tops (which I always removed before driving to class). I upgraded my wardrobe the best I could, scouring the racks at Marshalls and other discount stores for brand-name shirts and ties to wear to mandatory mass. On a trip to Mexico, I bought a fake Rolex to complement my new look. I exchanged my inexpensive sunglasses for Ray-Bans, shelling out more than three-fourths of a Pete's paycheck for a pair. Between my new car payment and my shopping sprees, my paychecks were quickly consumed; the installation of a car phone in my Pulsar nearly broke the bank.

A little research had proven that you had to have credit in order to get a phone installed in your car. I knew my parents would balk at the idea, so I turned to a fellow coworker, offering to spot him fifty on top of the installation fee if he would cosign on the account. My coworker agreed, cautioning me about what he'd do if I didn't pay my monthly phone bills and ruined his credit. I promised I would pay and made the necessary arrangements. I nearly wrecked the car glancing down at the small black protuberance installed next to the shifter, the orange buttons on the phone lit like a jack-o'-lantern. My first call was to Pete's, to tell my boss I was running a little late. After my boss hung up, I held the phone in my right hand while steering with my left, pretending to talk as cars whooshed past me on the freeway.

.

It soon became apparent that my Pete's paychecks were not enough to support my new lifestyle. The few dollars remaining after my car payment and monthly cellular bill left me with little cash to flaunt, so I began skimming the classifieds for a second job. A position as a part-time file clerk in a downtown law firm piqued my curiosity, and I arranged an interview for a Friday, which was mass day, so that I wouldn't have to change clothes in the bathroom after school.

The law firm was located a few miles from Brophy, less than a five-minute drive down Central Avenue. The cool air rushed past me as I pushed through the heavy double glass doors and stepped into the quiet office. The receptionist took my name and courteously offered me a seat in the tastefully decorated living room. A woman with short hair and a curt manner appeared in the hall behind the receptionist, sizing me up. Thinking it was the office manager, I smiled hello, but the woman didn't smile back and disappeared down the hall. I smoothed my Oscar de la Renta tie over my white shirt, unhooking my cuff from under my fake Rolex.

A young woman introduced herself and asked me to follow her into the file room. Her mother was the office manager, as it turned out, and she was detained in another part of the building but joined us a few moments later. My interview consisted of a roundtable discussion about Brophy, and about lawyers, and about Pete's Fish & Chips (which they loved). They hired me at the end of the interview, setting my schedule for Tuesdays, Wednesdays, and Thursdays after school. By the time I calculated the paltry number of hours times minimum wage, I was too absorbed with the idea of working side by side with lawyers in a fancy high-rise along Central Avenue to care. That my new employment robbed me of hours previously spent with Jenny was a graver concern, but as she had done since my transfer to Brophy, Jenny supported me and we vowed to grab every extra minute we could to be together.

The perks associated with my new job made themselves known immediately. The firm consisted of just two lawyers, the curt woman from earlier, a Stanford graduate, and an older man whom I nicknamed the Barrister because he'd graduated from Oxford. That the Barrister and Grim Face were partners was a bit of a mystery, since their offices were at opposite ends of the hall and they screamed things to each other, rather than strolling into the other's office for a conference. I sensed the competition between them and knew to be careful about their playing me off each other.

Still, it was too hard to say no when the Barrister asked me if I minded doing a couple of personal errands. I said I didn't; the reward was the keys to his Mercedes, which he wanted to have washed. Parked in the small garage under the building, the Mercedes sedan was crowded on either side, and I walked around the parking space to measure the distance between the neighboring cars. A cement pillar in the rearview mirror indicated just how tricky the situation was. The dash lit up as I turned the ignition; I watched the power antenna rise. I sank into the smooth leather driver's seat and positioned myself so that I could easily look over my shoulder as I backed out, rather than trusting the rearview mirror. The car performed sluggishly, perhaps sensing that the driver was not its owner, and I perfected the twenty-point turn as I finally nosed the Mercedes toward the light. The car popped up on Central Avenue and I hesitated, waiting for the right opening in traffic, then finally merged into the lane closest to me, the car seeming to hold back as I accelerated. It wasn't until I approached the car wash that I realized I'd mistaken the emergency brake indicator light on the dashboard for some cool German iconography. I released the emergency brake and pulled into the open channel at the car wash, pretending the car was mine as I gave instructions for its cleaning to the car wash employee, who nodded dutifully and called me sir. I was already casting the desired perception, founded as it was on nothing.

Though the hours I worked at the law firm were a mere third of the hours I worked at Pete's, I began answering the question about where I worked by telling people of my job on Central Avenue only. I liked the way people's eyes lit up when I mentioned the word "lawyer," and I especially liked the impression it gave of me as a Young Man on the Rise. There are few professions that people have a general admiration for, and I quickly learned that being a lawyer was one of them, so I took to reading as much as I could when my duties as file clerk expanded to include research. I imagined my knowledge of the law gaining on that of the two lawyers whose names were etched on the glass door, and incorporated the phrase "legally speaking" into my daily vocabulary. I was well on my way, I thought, and was sorely disappointed when Grim Face sent word that I needed to wear dressier clothes to work. Embarrassed, but also angry that I wasn't making enough to wear better clothes, I told the office manager I'd comply, knowing once I left for the day, I wouldn't ever return, my legal apprenticeship expiring as quietly as it had begun.

•

I was convinced that Jay Gatsby was me, and Jenny was Daisy, and it wasn't money that was keeping us apart, but Mormonism. And so my decision to join the Mormon Church was borne not out of religious zeal but out of romantic sacrifice. I kept my plan to be baptized Mormon a secret at first; Jenny was wary when I asked to start attending church with her and her family, sensing my motive. "You don't have to," she said, though I knew she was thrilled about having me in the pews on Sunday.

Persuading first the bishop, and then the elders assigned to my religious study, was a matter of simple playacting. Their collective need to believe in me was the same impulse that had drawn them to religion, I guessed. There were moments during the endless conversations with the elders about the tenets of Mormonism when I felt guilty, or at the very least fraudulent, but they and their religion were only an obstacle to my future happiness with Jenny.

After some months of study, the day of my baptism finally

arrived. I'd chosen Jenny's father to perform the ritual, which involved full immersion in a tub of water. Having arrived early Sunday morning, I sat in my car in the parking lot, the gravity of what I was about to do occurring to me for the first time. The absence of any family or close friends would not be a signal to the other members of the congregation, as no one in Jenny's circle knew anything about my private life.

After my cleansing by water, I ascended the pulpit. My eyes teared as a surprise homily about the importance of love issued forth, though I avoided Jenny's eyes, afraid of exposure as a fraud.

•

My gloating at having vanquished the sole stumbling block to a future with Jenny, just as Gatsby did when he reversed his personal fortunes in order to be with Daisy, was interrupted by a class assignment: Our American history class was visited by a local television sportscaster, J.D. Hayworth, who used the appearance to try out his new ambition—politics. (Hayworth would go on to serve as a congressman from Arizona's Fifth Congressional District.) Hayworth beseeched us to get involved with local politics, and our teacher offered extra credit for those who volunteered for either the Democratic senator Dennis DeConcini's reelection campaign or for the Republican challenger Keith DeGreen's bid to unseat DeConcini. The fact that Senator DeConcini had opened his campaign headquarters across the street from Brophy ensured that most of my classmates would spend time stuffing envelopes or answering phones for the Democratic incumbent. I had grown up in an apolitical house, so the difference between a Democratic and a Republican seemed to me to be nothing more than semantics, an idea that was reinforced when I learned that Keith DeGreen was in fact a lifelong Democrat who had simply changed parties in order to challenge DeConcini and realize his personal ambition. In a show of contrarianism, I decided to throw my lot in with the DeGreen campaign, which I quickly learned was composed of one other staffer, DeGreen's son Keith Jr., who had dropped out of the University of Arizona to help run his father's campaign.

Keith Jr. met me for lunch at the Wendy's on Camelback Road, and he laid out the campaign's main objective: to get the word out about his father's campaign by posting signage around town that boasted the would-be Senator DeGreen's profile. He produced a xeroxed map of the surrounding area that he'd marked up with red Xs, indicating the work we had in front of us.

The first order of business was to retrieve the manual auger for digging the holes for the signposts from his father's house. Keith Jr. had just come from the signage company, and his Jeep Wagoneer was loaded down with signs and posts. I followed him up Camelback Road, amazed as we sailed through the entrance to the Biltmore Estates, an exclusive development built around the Frank Lloyd Wright–inspired Arizona Biltmore Hotel. The hotel had hosted every president going back to Herbert Hoover, as well as Hollywood royalty like Jimmy Stewart; and Irving Berlin wrote "White Christmas" poolside at one of the resort's many luxurious pools.

Keith DeGreen's house was not one of the mansions circling the golf course but was a smaller affair inside one of the gated communities, Taliverde. Keith Jr. motioned back at me, and the guard let both vehicles pass. The DeGreen abode was a single-level patio home with a splash of grass out front. Keith Jr. invited me inside while he made a couple of non-campaign-related phone calls, instructing me to help myself to anything in the refrigerator. I grabbed a Coke and remained in the cool kitchen, the dark wood cabinets and black countertops seeming to dim the day into night. A deep emptiness pervaded the house, the kitchen stacked with supplies purchased in bulk but not stored away.

"Okay," Keith Jr. said, reappearing suddenly. "You can leave your car. We'll take mine."

We loaded up the auger and set out for the first red X on the map, the corner of North Twenty-Fourth Street and East Lincoln Drive, a mile or so away from the DeGreen residence. Keith Jr. steered his Wagoneer off the pavement and onto the undeveloped rocky terrain along East Lincoln Drive. It was quickly decided (by Keith Jr.) that I would dig the holes for the posts and he would attach the signs once the posts were firmly in the ground. The traffic at the busy intersection whooshed by as I grappled with the auger, the unforgiving ground resisting the tool. The excavation was slowgoing, and it took the better part of the afternoon to erect our first sign, the green-and-white billboard faced strategically, in plain view for all registered voters to see.

My first day volunteering for the DeGreen campaign was also my last. It took only a couple of missed phone calls for me to lose interest in the extra-credit assignment (or who would be elected to the Senate from Arizona, and I gave the results only a passing nod—DeConcini was reelected by what was considered a narrow margin), quickly realizing that political power was assigned arbitrarily, an idea that was less interesting than the romantic nature of power.

•

Ajay, a fellow Brophy Bronco, invited me to ditch class and and go with the other Young Republicans to attend a rally for President Reagan, who was speaking in Tempe at Arizona State University. As we motored off campus, I admired the leather interior of his sleek black Mercedes 190E. A Young Republican sitting up front grabbed the car phone off its cradle and called in a pizza, which we picked up on our way to Tempe, and the squad of us happily munched away as Ajay cranked the radio. I felt more like Nick Carraway than Jay Gatsby, but I enjoyed the afternoon excursion into the upper echelon, if only for the day.

•

My relationship with Jenny began to feel like a separate life, one with a separate set of friends and activities (church dances, cards and board games at her house, or the occasional date allowed by my work schedule now that she was sixteen). The natural ease we felt being together convinced me that the relationship was solid and that we were destined for each other. But the fact that I hardly talked about her when I was with my family, who still didn't know much about her, or my friends, who knew her about as well and saw her even less, drove a wedge in that serenity.

Dan Cody

That's me at the conference table with two FBI agents, the seat still warm from Teddy, who had finished his interview a few moments earlier, his last question to the agents, "Should I engage an attorney?" jangling my nerves.

The summer after graduation proved a watershed time. My idea to enroll in summer classes at Arizona State University to gain a head start on my college career evaporated the moment I moved into an apartment in Tempe with my old Tolleson High band section leader and our mutual friend Ty. We'd been inseparable at Tolleson and had remained in touch after they went away to college. The social life as a junior and senior at Brophy had never materialized, so my off-hours had been spent at college parties with my old high school friends. Our apartment in Tempe was a tiny affair—I slept at the foot of my old section leader's bed until Ty moved into the dorms in the fall—but I welcomed our reunion.

I continued in my capacity as night manager at the Pete's in Tolleson, leaving my apartment early to drive to Jenny's house to spend time with her before my four o'clock shift, which was sometimes a struggle owing to my late nights with

Ty and my old section leader at after-hours clubs like Out of Water, Six Feet Under, and Asylum. We favored Out of Water, a small bar on the outskirts of town, loading my old section leader's Volkswagen bus with beer and drinking in the darkened parking lot without fear of the police, entertaining various bar patrons who invited themselves into the bus's living-room area for a beer.

I also attended church services with Jenny and her family on Sundays, though I continued to work on Sundays as well. Sundays proved the worst day of the week, coming as they did at the end of what were usually full weekends involving long work shifts, late nights, and me bouncing back and forth between Tempe and Tolleson, driving the thirty miles each way as many as six times in the space of seventy-two hours. Much to my surprise, I was able to maintain these two disparate lifestyles, though I concealed from Jenny how I spent Friday and Saturday nights after work. The fact that I would never run into any of her friends in these after-hours clubs emboldened me to lie, and I was able to convince even myself that I went home after work and slept rather than slathering my hair with gel, dressing in black, and spinning until four in the morning on a dance floor, then hanging out in the parking lot afterward, sometimes seeing the sun rise.

The start of my first year at college demanded an alteration of my summer schedule; everything was scaled back to allow for my eight o'clock classes, my schedule loaded with early classes so that I could have some study time in the afternoon before I trekked to Tolleson to put in seven hours at Pete's. My studies quickly began suffering—as did my sleep—and so scanning the employment board at Arizona State

University became part of my daily routine. After four years of late nights toiling in grease, I was ready to leave Pete's Fish & Chips for something else. The part-time job in the downtown law firm my junior year had left me with research, filing, and general office skills sufficient enough to be considered for similar jobs, so I narrowed my search to law firms. (As an English major, I labored under the illusion that I would eventually find myself in law school.) Every morning on my way to eight o'clock Latin class, I would swoop by the job board to view the fresh postings. The job descriptions were generally the same: "So-and-so seeks well-organized person to help with office duties. Some typing. Must have own vehicle." The pay was generally the same too, an hourly amount that hovered just above minimum wage, which was why the posting by American Continental Corporation seeking a runner for seven dollars an hour stood out. The posting stood out too because I knew that American Continental owned Lincoln Savings and Loan, as well as the Phoenician, a world-class luxury hotel built into the side of Camelback Mountain (the marble used in the lobby had been mined from the same quarry in Italy that had supplied the marble Michelangelo used for the Pietà), all of which was owned and operated by one Charles H. Keating Jr., who was the target of a government investigation over the multibillion-dollar failure of Lincoln. And then there was the separate investigation into the so-called Keating Five—Dennis DeConcini (D-AZ), John McCain (R-AZ), Alan Cranston (D-CA), John Glenn (D-OH), and Don Riegle (D-MI)—who had received over a million dollars collectively in campaign contributions from Charlie and who were accused of improperly interceding with the government on Charlie's behalf. When asked if he expected special treatment in return for his political contributions, the flamboyant developer replied, "I want to say in the most forceful way I can: I certainly hope so."

I'd heard of Charlie Keating before his name became a regular fixture in the papers, though. Brophy College Prep boasted a Keating Hall, the honor bestowed after Charlie donated a nice sum toward the construction of Brophy's library. Charlie also regularly placed in the top ten of the Phoenix 40, an annual compilation of the forty wealthiest and most influential businessmen (whose sons invariably attended Brophy). Certain titillating rumors about Charlie reached the populace via profiles in newspapers and local magazines: that he hopped between real estate properties by helicopter; that he kept a private plane in a hangar at Sky Harbor International; that he hired only young, staggeringly beautiful secretaries, who were collectively known as Charlie's Angels.

I had all of this in mind—along with the fact that James Gatz apprenticed himself to Dan Cody on his way to becoming Jay Gatsby—when I borrowed a jacket from my old section leader and drove to American Continental Corporation for an interview.

ACC's offices on Camelback Road consisted of a two-story building for administration (top floor) and legal (bottom floor), and a single-story building that housed accounting. An impeccably manicured driveway separated the buildings, the asphalt tributary running around back to the employee parking lot, each space carefully stenciled with the initials of the space's owner. At the far end of the parking lot, a basketball hoop mingled with the fronds from a neighboring palm tree, which was undergoing pruning by the team of Tongan land-scapers imported from the archipelago of South Pacific islands by Charlie himself, all outfitted in turquoise polo shirts bearing the Phoenician's logo.

"Good costume," someone said, pointing at my borrowed jacket, as I walked through the parking lot. "Love the Blues Brothers." The comment meant nothing to me until I walked into the reception area and was greeted by the receptionist, who was dressed as the devil, replete with plastic tail and pitchfork.

It occurred to me then that it was Halloween.

The receptionist invited me to wait in a nearby conference room, showing me to a couch flanked by towers of boxes. Through the floor-to-ceiling drapes I could see men in suits sauntering through the hallways. The electronic buzz of the switchboard was nearly constant.

The conference room door clicked opened and a man in his early seventies appeared, closing the door behind him. "Hello," he said, introducing himself as Dr. Theodore F. Weber. "You can call me Teddy." Teddy asked me a few questions about myself, genuinely interested in the answers. Eager to talk about the job, I mentioned that Charlie had made a generous donation to my high school. "That's the kind of man he is," Teddy said enthusiastically. "If you come to work for us, you'll see that for yourself. The thing is this: We all work for Mr. Keating. He's the captain of the team, and everything belongs to him—the bats, the balls, the playing field, everything. And we're his team." That was the closest we'd get to discussing the job. Instead we diverged into the fact that Teddy had come to work for Charlie through his son-in-law, who worked at Lincoln, after running a successful medical practice in Chicago. He'd moved with his wife to Scottsdale to be closer to his daughter and had magically been tapped by Charlie to head up the runner department, the backbone of ACC.

"So when can you start?" Teddy asked.

I said I'd have to give two weeks' notice at my job.

"Oh, I'm afraid we'll need someone before that," he said.

"Okay," I said. "How about a week's notice, then? I can start next Monday."

"Fine," Teddy said. "That'll be fine."

A week later to the day, I was American Continental's newest runner, a position I learned had an amorphous set of responsibilities. There were certain absolutes: The three supply rooms, one on each floor, were to be inventoried and restocked daily; the out-of-state lawyers fighting Charlie's various legal wars were to be shuttled to the airport on Friday afternoons and picked up again on Monday mornings; a catered lunch was to be provided daily on each floor, every entrée from a different restaurant (Charlie's theory about this was that if he catered lunch, the lawyers were less likely to disappear for hours in the afternoon); the mail was to be run three times daily between ACC and the Phoenician, where Charlie had his office (Charlie maintained an office at ACC, too, but he'd abandoned it for the Italian marble and glass chandeliers of the Phoenician); the buildings were to be opened at 7 a.m. and closed at 7 p.m. I came to understand that the largest responsibility, by far, was to be ready to be called into action should the need arise: a last-minute run to FedEx, spinning one of the family's Mercedeses through the local car wash, beating the clock at the courthouse clerk's office with a legal filing, etc.

My first day on the job, I was certain I'd made a serious error in judgment.

"We could lose our jobs any day," my fellow runner Trish said on one of the mail runs to the Phoenician. "We're all just waiting to get fired. A lot of people have already quit."

Trish's grim prediction spooked me. I'd traded a forty-hour-a-week job at a decent wage for a thirty-hour-a-week job that paid less money, hoping that I'd quickly rise through the ranks to more hours and more money. The possibility that the opposite would happen was a disaster, and I reintroduced the scan of the employment board into my daily routine, in the event that I came to work at ACC one day to find the doors locked. These daily perusals revealed what I thought was a brilliant solution to what wasn't yet a real problem: The law library on campus was hiring for ten or twelve hours a week at minimum wage. The job was simple—working the front desk and doing occasional shelving—and I envisioned getting paid to study for my classes as I sat quietly at the front desk. I interviewed for the position less than thirty minutes after seeing the posting and was hired to start that night by the library manager, a woman in her thirties who had no real interest in the law but was dedicated to proper shelving techniques and maintaining the quiet so that the law students scurrying about would have the right environment in which to pursue their studies. The job would provide the necessary piece of the precarious employment bridge I was building and reawakened certain platonic conceptions of myself as one of the great lawyers of the land. My first night behind the desk bore these feelings out as I spent my shift familiarizing myself with the stacks, noting the difference between the Federal Reporter, which contained U.S. Court of Appeals cases, and the Federal Supplement, which contained U.S. District Court cases. Learning how to read legal citations like 743 F. Supp. 901 (volume 743 of the Federal Supplement, page 901) empowered me with the false sense that I had a rudimentary understanding of the law, a skill I dreamed about falling back on if things with Charlie Keating didn't pan out.

·

Access to Charlie's attorneys during airport runs was a source of inside information as to how the fight was going—it was always hard to tell from the runners' den what was really going on—but also provided a glimpse into their personalities. Flying back and forth between L.A. and Phoenix for a high-profile client like Charlie and staying at the Phoenician for free seemed like the pinnacle of any legal career, so I was shocked when the lead attorney lamented his choice of law school over veterinary school as I shuttled him to the airport to catch a plane home to Beverly Hills. His Rolex flashed as he gestured about his love for animals, and while at first I thought he was putting me on, I soon realized that he was nothing but sincere, and it sucked the wind out of the sail of my ambitions to be a lawyer, just like that.

•

One morning a few weeks into my new employment at ACC, I arrived to find a caravan of moving trucks idling like overheated camels in the driveway. ACC executives cautiously maneuvered their Mercedeses and Porsches around the moving men, who were unloading office furniture, artwork, plants, and pottery.

"Mr. Keating is back," Teddy said in answer to my question. By lunch I'd learned that the government had seized the Phoenician and expelled its monarch and his inner circle, executives who were related to Charlie either by blood or by marriage. Suddenly names I'd previously seen only in newspapers or on the mail I delivered thrice daily to the Phoenician were wandering the halls. The noose seemed to be tightening—first the government had seized Lincoln, including the Phoenix office, which adjoined ACC on Camelback Road, separated only by a short sidewalk between the two buildings (part of my daily responsibilities was to separate the mail addressed to Lincoln, call the guard service, and then walk ten steps out the back door of the runners' den to make the switch for mail addressed to ACC), now the Phoenician—and I imagined that these losses, chronicled daily in the media, were a source of embarrassment for Charlie.

Clearing out one of the empty offices for a new occupant, I stumbled across a box of yellow buttons emblazoned with the declaration i like charlie keating, which had been used at an innocuous real estate event sometime prior to the bankruptcy. I fastened a button to my shirt and squirreled the rest away in my desk for reserve.

The button raised my profile immediately, not just within, but without. The office personnel at the courthouse suddenly knew my name, as did the chefs at the upscale restaurants that catered our lunches. "Hey, it's Charlie's man," the temps who had been hired to scan hundreds of thousands of documents onto microfilm greeted me. I liked the association and suffered through the raised eyebrows and smirks I encountered as I ran errands in the city—we runners had grown used to the honks and middle fingers in traffic as we zoomed through the streets in vans marked with the American Continental logo—though I couldn't imagine any thinking person taking the government's side in this monumental struggle. (More than likely, people simply associated Charlie with the $3.4 billion taxpayers would have to fork over because of Lincoln's failure, the single highest price tag in the $200 billion S&L debacle.)

My new designation as Charlie's number one booster brought with it unsought confidences. Probably the most scurrilous rumor I heard associated with Charlie stemmed from his well-publicized battle with Larry Flynt. In July 1976, Flynt was arrested and charged with pandering, obscenity, and organized crime. Flynt was convicted on all counts and sentenced to $11,000 in fines and seven to twenty-five years in prison. However, less than a week later, Flynt filed a successful appeal, thumbing his nose at Charlie and his organization, Citizens for Decency through Law (CDL). A year or so later, Flynt was shot twice on the opening day of another obscenity trial, this time in Georgia. The teller of the rumor raised his eyebrows as he related the anecdote to me in a lowered voice, inviting me to connect the dots.

Tales of Charlie's generosity outweighed innuendo, though. There was the one about him taking all the secretaries to Beverly Hills for an afternoon shopping spree; the one about how Charlie bought an old elementary school and remodeled it as a swim club, swimming being a passion that ran in the Keating family (Charlie was an avid swimmer, and his son, Charles H. Keating III, had swum in the Olympics, as did Charlie's son-in-law Gary Hall Sr. and his grandson Gary Hall Jr.); or how Charlie donated generously to Mother Teresa (his corporate jet was at her disposal). That Charlie was being generous with other people's money was an easy charge to level, but there was something seductive about his desire to give, which I guessed was fed by his want to be liked.

·

I envisioned myself a foot soldier under Charlie's command.

And no job was too small.

When Charlie needed someone to fetch a tie from his modest but gorgeous house, I volunteered, punching in the gate code (Charlie's anniversary date) and letting myself into the empty house. My worn loafers clicked against the marble floor as I soaked in the spectacular view of the desert from the bay windows in the kitchen. Charlie's house was perched on a large expanse of desert property, he and Mrs. Keating on one end, their daughter and her husband living in the more sumptuous Spanish-mission-style home (with Olympic-size swimming pool) on the other. I traipsed through the tastefully decorated living room (furnished with the same style and color of furniture as the Phoenician and ACC offices) into the master bedroom, a space as large as the front room. I posed in the bathroom mirror and ran my fingers through my hair, admiring my i like charlie keating button, marveling at my infiltration of such a nice house. I thought about how my ghostly footprints would never be known by Charlie or any of the fabulous people who most certainly came through Charlie's front door, how once I stepped back out into the driveway, it would be like I'd never been there.

I finally met Charlie Keating face-to-face the second time I paid a visit to his manse, some two months after I started working at ACC. Charlie sometimes liked to walk the few miles between the office and his house for exercise (shrugging off the concerns for his safety from coworkers and colleagues), and so one of the runners would drive his Mercedes to his house at lunch, with a runner in a company vehicle following. As I was the last hire, the lead position in this two-car caravan was never offered to me; but one day Charlie walked home without notifying anyone, then called for his car after all the other runners had gone home, save me and my fellow runner Trish. Trish had no interest in driving Charlie's Mercedes (she was afraid she'd wreck it), and so I confidently took the keys from Teddy, barely hearing his warning to be careful.

I had, to that moment, driven every car in the Keating fleet except Charlie's Mercedes. Once every week or so, two runners would spend an entire day driving the company cars through the car wash that was a mile or so away, including the company's two identical tan Cadillac limousines, which sat like sleeping tigers in the back of the employee parking lot. But I'd never been closer to Charlie's Mercedes than passing it in the parking lot (it was the first in the row of employee parking, closest to the door and directly in sight of Charlie's office window, so I rarely stopped to admire it). It was like no Mercedes I'd ever seen, and there was a rumor that it had been imported. The dark-blue interior matched the custom paint job, and I had to adjust the driver's seat to account for the difference between Charlie's six-feet-two frame and my five-feet-eleven reach. I carefully started the immaculate car, the dashboard and stereo lighting up as I surveyed the gauges and Charlie's preset radio stations. After adjusting the rearview mirror (but not the side mirrors; I couldn't figure out how), I backed the car out of its spot and pulled into traffic, Trish behind me in one of the company vans.

The drive up Camelback Road to Charlie's house was a short one, but I savored every mile, the Mercedes floating along the streets, veering softly with the slightest turn of the steering wheel, as if the machine were reading my mind. I eased the car into Charlie's driveway, punched in the gate code, and touched the accelerator to climb the sharp incline. My instructions were to leave the keys in the car, but I recognized my chance and strolled through the marble portico and knocked on the solid wood of the front door. Trish threw her hands in the air and shrugged, and I smiled back.

The heavy door swung open and Charlie stood towering over me, beaming, his jacket and tie replaced with a polo shirt bearing the Phoenician logo.

"I . . . I brought your car," I said, stammering, caught without anything to say.

"Great!" Charlie said. "Do you want something to drink?" He stepped aside to let me in.

"Who is it?" a voice asked. Mrs. Keating, a smallish, impeccably groomed woman, appeared from the kitchen. "Oh, hello."

"This is Jaime," Charlie said. "He's a good guy." Charlie slapped me on the back with a force that propelled me forward.

"Very nice to meet you," Mrs. Keating said.

"Here are the keys," I said dumbly.

Mrs. Keating disappeared into the kitchen and Charlie followed her, then reappeared with two cans of soda. "For the road," he said. I took the cans, wanting instead to be invited for dinner, to eat from expensive china and hear conversations littered with references to Charlie's friends: Ivan Boesky, the Wall Streeter who was eventually busted for insider trading; Michael Milken, the genius junk bond financier at Drexel Burnham whom the government charged with securities violations (my economics teacher at Brophy, a former broker at Drexel, first introduced me to the idea of junk bonds, and to the name Michael Milken; he began every class by pulling a bottle of Pepto-Bismol from his leather briefcase and chugging a healthy swig); or Sir James Goldsmith, the billionaire merchant banker. I relished the idea of annotating this fantasy dinner conversation with what little I knew about high finance, indicating gently that I was willing to learn, wanted to be an apprentice.

The Boat in Little Girl Bay

That's me in Unalaska, hefting a bag of trash over the side of our vessel, the cool fresh air flushing the stale ship air from my lungs. I wondered what chores James Gatz had aboard Dan Cody's boat when it left Little Girl Bay, before he learned what he learned from Cody and changed his name to Jay Gatsby. A week into my new job on an Alaskan fishing boat and I still didn't feel any relief from the anxieties that had chased me all the way from Phoenix.

My girlfriend, Jenny, had felt the pinch too. She would never accuse, but it had been clear that our relationship was third on the list of my priorities, and we both knew it could slip further. I was at a loss for what to do. If I'd felt like I was living two lives in high school, the feeling was tripled in college. Jenny knew nothing of my fellow employees at American Continental; she had visited my apartment in Tempe only once, having been forbidden to do so by her mother. The converse was true too. I didn't closely follow what was happening her senior year at Tolleson, a negligence I knew was unfair. And for the first time, the emotional bond between us seemed strained. Worse, I felt the continuing grip of the forward propulsion that had marked my entire life. Against my dire wishes, I was on the move again. All of which was why I agreed to drive out to her house the Friday after midterms—the spring semester brought with it a fresh start academically—to celebrate my surviving the arduous tests and to reconnect the wires of our relationship.

That Friday was as eventful as it was stressful. I took my final midterm that morning and arrived late for work at ACC to find a series of court filings waiting for me, Charlie's fight to regain control of Lincoln Savings and Loan from the government heating up. I raced to the courthouse, barely beating the filing deadline. I realized too late that I'd forgotten to renew my car insurance, the insurance office having closed at five. Since the bank held the lien to my car, I knew I'd have to renew the insurance first thing Monday morning if I wanted to avoid a mess of trouble. I decided to spend Sunday night at home, to be closer to the insurance office, a plan that wouldn't see fruition. After an uncomfortable evening trying to re-create one of our many good times watching movies and playing pool in her living room, it was clear a chasm had opened up between Jenny and me. I could barely keep my eyes open during the movie and catnapped my way to midnight, the curfew her mother had set for my visits. We hugged and kissed good night, and I sensed that she was relieved that I was going. I didn't bother replacing the T-tops on my car, hoping the cold night air would keep me awake. Instead the whoosh of rushing air lulled me to sleep, and I remember wondering two things simultaneously: How had I gotten off the freeway, and why was a Suburban stopped in front of me? I applied the brakes, too late to avoid sliding under the Suburban's bumper, my hood buckling as my seat belt caught, knocking the wind out of me, the windshield cracking violently.

I jumped out of my car, the radio still blaring, to face the driver of the Suburban, who asked if I was okay. Adrenaline kept me upright until the paramedics arrived, and it wasn't until I was laid out on a stretcher on the sidewalk that the gravity of the situation descended upon me. A quick trip to the emergency room confirmed that nothing was broken, but the ER wouldn't release me on my own, so I called my apartment, the phone ringing and ringing and ringing, my old section leader somewhere off in the night. I hung up and called K——, a friend of my old section leader who worked at a futon store and had sold us our futon at a five-finger discount, the only other person whose number I could remember, hoping he'd know where my old section leader was. K—— was not happy to hear from me, but when I told him where I was, he drove down to pick me up, with a girl who looked equally chagrined riding in the passenger's side. K—— agreed to run me by the all-night pharmacy so I could fill my prescription for painkillers (I dropped him a couple of pills as a thank-you), and K—— and the girl rode the pharmacy's plastic pony indecently while we waited. Without my keys, which had been towed away with my broken car, I couldn't get into my empty apartment, so K—— drove me back to his place and I crashed on the couch, K—— and the girl retreating to his bedroom, picking up where they'd left off.

I spent the weekend in a medically induced fog, dreading telling my parents not that I'd wrecked my car, but that I'd let the insurance lapse. Gatsby claimed his relations were all dead so as to complete his own self-invention. When Gatsby's father showed up at his funeral, the father continued to be a believer in Gatsby and his ambitions. My own parents had communicated their belief in me in similar ways, so it was an agitation to fail to live up to the autonomy I'd been granted. My father helped me try to fix the damage, so that the insurance company wouldn't know. We bought the Suburban driver's silence for five hundred dollars.

The third shoe that dropped in that short span of time was a legal ruling against Charlie's bid to reacquire Lincoln Savings, the U.S. District Court judge ruling that Charlie's management of Lincoln had amounted to Charlie looting the savings and loan as if it were his own personal piggy bank. The ruling cast a pall over American Continental, and an ever-increasing number of Charlie's supporters found employment elsewhere. I realized that I needed to do the same—in addition to my regular bills (car payments, rent, etc.), I now had to contend with the three thousand dollars it would take to fix my car—and so I looked for another job.

Combing through the classified ads in the State Press, the campus newspaper, I spotted the ad I was looking for: "$PEND THE $UMMER IN ALA$KA." I dialed the toll number, dreaming of the riches that awaited at the other end of the line. Everyone knew someone who knew someone who had gone to Alaska for the summer only to return with the spending power of a Midas or Rockefeller. Surely the fish trade could support one more hard worker down on his luck. It was just the kind of scheme James Gatz would've undertaken, I presumed.

The number in the ad did not provide jobs in Alaska, however, but for twenty of my last dollars I could purchase a directory of canneries and fishing companies that would (maybe might, who knows?) employ me for the summer. The operator who took my credit card number failed to inform me that, it being May, all the jobs were likely already booked, a fact I discovered only after receiving the directory and phoning (on the company dime) my way through most of the alphabetical entries.

Finally a friendly voice informed me that, yes, there was an opening on a vessel that had just pulled into port, an image that sounded terribly romantic. However, I would have to fly out immediately in order to set sail with the crew, who had come in to change the fishing nets to comply with the government-regulated fishing seasons.

I accepted the offer, borrowed a company van to run a few errands (including shaving my head), gave notice, said goodbye, and called Jenny and my family, who hastily joined me at Sky Harbor International for a brief farewell. Jenny seemed aggrieved that I was leaving, which I (mistakenly) took as a sign of hope for our future.

The first leg of the flight, from Phoenix to Salt Lake City, felt like bail jumping. I was leaving my problems behind but also undertaking their correction. After an hour-long layover, I boarded the next flight and fell asleep. I woke sometime before our landing in Anchorage. The eternal Alaskan sunlight lent an adventurous quality to my travels, and though I'd slept fitfully, I raced through the airport to my next connection, a commuter flight on a prop plane to Dutch Harbor, a port on Unalaska, one of the middle Aleutian Islands.

The shack at the end of the single-lane landing strip—which was in fact the Unalaska Airport—ground my sense of adventure to a halt. Where was I and how did I get here? Wasn't it only hours earlier that I had been surrounded by my family and Jenny, nervously laughing about my sudden summer employment? Who were these two Norwegians with the rusted pickup truck, motioning that we should get going? And where was my bag?

The Norwegians did not speak English, and so after some pantomiming, one of them went off in search of my luggage. I excused myself and pretended to dial home on the pay phone in the airport lobby. I faked a conversation with my father that began with my informing him that I had arrived, then contorted my face when I heard the phantom news that one of my beloved brothers had just been in a serious car wreck. I looked over to make sure that the intended audience was watching my performance before hanging up.

"I'm sorry," I said to the Norwegians, who had just told me through a series of gestures and monosyllabic words that my bag did not make it from Anchorage. "My brother has been in a car wreck. I need to go home."

The Norwegians seemed to understand the word "home," though they motioned toward their idling truck. I recognized my limited options. I could refuse to get in the truck and take my chances, but the Unalaska Airport did not feature any airport hotels (and I wasn't traveling with any money anyway), so I climbed in the middle of the bench seat and we tooled our way toward the harbor, the airport receding behind us until it was out of sight.

This won't be so bad, I told myself as we cruised through the harbor. The ships were enormous, and maybe it would be fun after all. I shook the panic with a visible shudder and then apologized for my behavior in the airport, an apology my Norwegian friends seemed to understand. The one next to me on the passenger side smiled a pearly smile and slapped me on the knee.

Having boarded the plane in Phoenix in shorts and a T-shirt, I was considerably underdressed for the climate. My driver swung us by the fishing company's office, and I signed some paperwork that I didn't read, handed to me by a nice woman who reminded me of my grandmother. I was also outfitted with a navy-blue sweat suit, the words dutch harbor, ak ironed on in orange block letters down the left pant leg.

"The boat comes back in two weeks," the nice woman said. "Your bag is sure to be here when you return." Fool that I was, or perhaps grateful to make a friendly acquaintance that I could feel comfortable coming to in a crisis, I thought the sweat suit was a gift. But the nice woman casually mentioned that it would be deducted from my first paycheck.

We said our good-byes and good lucks and continued through the harbor. I noticed that the ships were growing considerably smaller, and the old panic returned. The truck stopped in front of the smallest trawler in the harbor, a boat that extended from here to there and looked like a less-than-mighty wind might capsize it. A crew of what appeared to be Americans was loading supplies onto the boat, and I was instructed to help.

Introductions were made, and it turned out that the crew was indeed mostly American. (I learned later that this was by design, as apparently in order for vessels to fish in American waters, a certain percentage of the crew must be native.) Two of the Americans had put the ship in the water somewhere off the coast of Washington and had sailed it to Dutch Harbor, a feat that drew my immediate admiration. I solicited the Americans about how much money I would make working the lines (i.e., gutting the fish hauled in by the ship's enormous netting apparatus that dragged the ocean floor) and was assured that it would be a substantial sum. The standard pay was 1 percent of the haul, but when talking about the size of the biweekly catch, one percent translated to thousands of dollars. Maybe tens of thousands.

Emboldened by this confirmation, I heartily pitched in. Once the supplies were loaded, I set out in search of the ship's captain to introduce myself. A series of fingers pointed me up a lattice of stairs that brought me to the captain's quarters, a faux-wood paneled room boldly decorated with centerfolds from racy European skin mags. I diverted my eyes long enough to look the captain in the face when we shook hands. The captain was Disneyesque in terms of proportion (and beard). He greeted me in his broken English, and it became clear that he wanted me to find the first mate in the pilothouse, which I did.

The first mate, a youngish man in his forties with an air of authority, spoke impeccable English. He indicated the satellite phone available for my use at ten dollars a minute (again to be deducted from my paycheck), and I immediately plotted a good time to call Jenny. The first mate then broke the bad news: The cook's helper had been promoted to the line, and the only position now open was in the kitchen at $4.25 an hour. I peered into the first mate's eyes, trying to ferret out the joke, and the first mate sensed my irritation.

"It's only for two weeks," he said. "When we go in again to change the nets, I'll get you on the line. I promise."

I didn't conceal my agitation, but nodded dumbly before trudging off to the kitchen to shake the cook's hand and receive a tour of the galley, whose most interesting feature was the fact that everything was secured to the wall or counter because of the listing while at sea.

I wouldn't see the cook for another two days, though. My first morning on the open water, I was gripped with a severe case of seasickness, opting to lie ramrod straight in my coffin-like bed stowed away in a closet-size room where I would live with my three other roommates. I dreamed of sunny desert days with Jenny, the golden sunlight dancing around us as we cruised around in my car with the T-tops off. I closed my eyes tight to avoid the reality that I was bobbing in a tin can somewhere close to Russian waters.

Eventually the cook sent the captain to my quarters to tell me plainly that I was needed in the kitchen. I nodded and joined the cook in his preparation of the daily meals. The main component of my new job was to crawl in the ship's bow, where the caught fish were packed and stored in ice after they were gutted, to retrieve the frozen packages of meats and vegetables stored among the ship's take. Another duty was trash removal, which became my favorite part of the day, as I was allowed to go above deck for a breath of fresh air while I tossed garbage bag after garbage bag into the ocean. And if it was the right time of day, I would watch the net hauled in, the mechanical apparatus slowly bringing up the day's dredge, which often included debris from the ocean floor (as well as fish caught out of season).

A week or so into the voyage, the captain indicated to me after dinner one night that he wanted me to clean the bathroom and shower used by the entire crew. I balked at the suggestion, a technique that had gotten me out of a similar request—that I be put in charge of the crew's laundry—but the captain insisted, and the entire dining room watched as I traipsed down the narrow hall toward the bathroom.

The ship rocked as I assessed the scene. Bits of toilet paper and half-used bars of soap littered the floor. Indignant at being publicly suborned, I grabbed the pressure washer hose from the nearby filleting area and turned it on the bathroom, spraying down the walls and stalls with a torrent of water too plentiful for the measly drain in the bathroom floor to handle.

I reported back to the captain that the bathroom was clean, and he barely interrupted his card game to acknowledge me.

What was really bothering me was not having to work in the kitchen for close to minimum wage, or being asked to clean the latrine, but the fact that my nightly ship-to-shore phone calls to Jenny were always answered by her mother, telling me that she was out, a story that grew less and less plausible as the days wore on. I should've embraced the narrative of two lovers being kept apart by distance and sea, though, because when I finally was able to raise Jenny on the phone, her icy tone bored a hole right through me.

"I'm thinking of coming home," I said.

"It's probably better if you stay," she said, which was all I needed to jump ship the moment we docked to change the nets and unload the haul, grabbing my bag—which was waiting for me upon my return—and hailing one of the cabs that ran up and down the pier.

The shack at the end of the runway was a welcome sight as

the cab dropped me off. The sky was filled with engine noise as a prop jet teetered in the sky, finally righting itself and sailing off into the horizon. I noted that the last flight out of Dutch Harbor was a mere four hours away and telephoned home for a ticket back to civilization, not realizing or caring that a no-advance one-way ticket from Dutch Harbor, Alaska, to Phoenix, Arizona, would only compound my financial troubles, the whole trip costing me money, in that I would never see my first and only paycheck (though between my ship-to-shore phone calls and my sweat suit, I would probably have realized very little profit). My father said he would do his best and told me to call back in an hour or so. I whiled the time away, leafing through a copy of People magazine that featured Christian Brando, who had apparently been arrested and booked on suspicion of murder.

A familiar face appeared on the horizon as I turned a page in the magazine. The ship's captain hurried toward me, his brow furrowed.

"I thought I'd find you here," he said in his halting English.

I shrugged. "Yeah, it's not working out," I said nervously. Could he force me to go back to the ship? And if my ticket didn't come through, wouldn't I need a place to stay anyway?

The captain nodded.

"I have to go home," I said, and saying it made me realize it was true. The captain nodded again and left without shaking hands or saying good-bye.

I was home a week before anyone knew I'd returned. An old high school friend finally called to say he'd heard I was back. I immediately rang Jenny, fearing she, too, knew of my return. I'd spent my week in solitary, puzzling over what to do about our relationship. I talked myself into taking a copy of The God Makers, an anti-Mormon film that I learned later was full of hateful inaccuracies, over to her house to try to convince her that her religion was bogus, blaming our problems directly on the fact that she was Mormon and that I was pretending to believe.

When I produced the tape of The God Makers, she looked at me like I was a complete stranger, like someone she had never known.

I knew then that I would never see her again.

•

As I'd been gone only a few weeks, I reclaimed my old job at American Continental. Everyone assumed I'd been on vacation and asked me how it was.

•

Upon my return, Teddy approached me about a mission Charlie wanted carried out. The days of American Continental were numbered, it seemed, and Charlie was making plans for life post-ACC, having rented office space up the road for a real estate consulting firm. Few knew that Charlie had handpicked a group of executives to move with him to this new venture (mostly family members), and he wanted to furnish the new office with items from the ACC offices. So as not to alarm those employees who were not in the know, the furniture would be moved before and after working hours, Mrs. Keating and others placing a small orange sticker on items that were to be moved up to the new offices.

Secrecy was an essential element of the transition, and Teddy deputized me and S——, another runner, for this very important responsibility. At first S—— and I moved effortlessly, making a run in the morning and one in the evening; the offices up the road filled quickly with expensive furniture. But then Charlie overestimated us, or perhaps forgot to consider who was facilitating his exodus, and a marble credenza S—— and I could barely lift wouldn't fit in the elevator.

"Should we even be doing this?" S—— asked me, exasperated. S—— had, from the outset, agreed to the mission simply because he wanted the overtime.

"I'm sure it's fine," I replied, unsure if it was or not.

"Then why do we have to sneak around like this?"

I smelled revolt and did my best to quell it. "Teddy wouldn't involve us in anything underhanded," I said, a truth S—— couldn't deny.

S—— waited with the credenza, which we parked in the atrium of the small office building, the other occupants glancing at it curiously as they filed in for another day at the office, while I called Teddy to apprise him of the situation. The twenty or so tenants seemed to know that Charlie Keating was moving into their building, and they watched from their windowed offices as S—— and I brought expensive piece after expensive piece through the front door, up the elevator, and down the hall to the newly rented corner office.

Teddy's instructions about the credenza did not make S—— happy.

"This is ridiculous," S—— said as I relayed Teddy's directive to take the credenza to the stables on Charlie's property.

The code for the back gate was the same as the code for the front, and we punched it in time and again, the gates opening slowly as we ferried the overflow of furniture to the stables. Three or four runs in, S—— asked to be relieved of his overtime duties, and Teddy took his place without comment, gabbing with the Tongans who landscaped Charlie's property while we unloaded our take in the crisp fall morning air. I hoped Charlie would remember my stamina when he made the move from ACC to his new office.

My interest was more than simple employment: If I could catch Charlie on his next upswing, everything would be fine, I guessed. Teddy revealed to me that once Charlie returned from making his initial appearance before Judge Lance Ito in a California courtroom on charges of fraud, racketeering, and conspiracy, we'd make the move to the new office. Charlie arrived at the office early that morning to meet with his Phoenix-based lawyers, who were handing him off to their L.A. counterparts upon his arrival later that day in California.

That I would never lay eyes on Charlie again did not occur to me as I dropped him off at the airport. The news bulletin at lunch about Charlie being taken into custody in Los Angeles at his initial appearance was a shock to us all. Chaos enveloped ACC in the wake of Charlie's incarceration, and the government acted quickly to install a trustee to ensure that their newly acquired assets were not mishandled by the executives related to Charlie by birth or marriage, who were debriefed and terminated in short order.

The government had caught wind of Charlie's new office up the road, and upon my early arrival one morning I was met with the unhappy news that the FBI wanted to talk to me and S—— and Teddy. In fact, Teddy was already being interviewed in the conference room in legal. I sprinted across the compound to find out what was going on, a wild look in my eye, bumping into WSR, a Southern lawyer who had the distinction of working at ACC both for Charlie and for the government. WSR had originally been employed by Wyman, Bautzer of Los Angeles, but he quit Wyman in a disagreement with the firm. The government then hired WSR to work with the trustee to help guide ACC's bankruptcy to completion.

"What is it?" he asked.

I explained to him what was happening, and he called me into his office and shut the door.

"What's the truth about the furniture?" he asked, sitting behind his desk.

I told him the whole story, about Charlie's new office, about the moving expeditions before and after work, about the stash of furniture in Charlie's stables. A horrified look clouded WSR's face. In the short time that I'd known him, I'd discerned that he was an aboveboard guy who did not tolerate dishonesty.

"My advice is to tell them the whole thing," he said. His words were not the legal comfort I was searching for. I wanted him to jump out from behind his desk, outraged, ready to defend me against the crush of a maniacal government run amok.

It occurred to me that I might be in real trouble, and I cursed Charlie for putting me in a vulnerable position.

The conference room doors swung open and a red-faced Teddy charged out, asking over his shoulder, "Should I engage an attorney?" The two young, fresh-faced FBI agents answered that that was up to him. Teddy spotted me coming out of WSR's office. "The boys had nothing to do with it," Teddy said.

"Thank you for your time," one of the agents said, motioning for me to take a seat at the conference table.

The legal conference room was a naturally dark room, its eastern exposure partially blocked by the accounting building across the compound. The FBI did not turn on the lights, but took their seats across the table from me. The credenza populated with tiny crystal tombstones commemorating ACC's various real estate transactions caught what light was available, twinkling like a constellation behind them.

"We already know from Teddy about your recent activities," the one agent said. "We just want to hear it from you."

The agent's use of Teddy's nickname frightened me. I'd seen such chummy tactics on television and knew that invariably they were employed only when questioning a doomed subject. One minute they'd have their arm around you, the next they'd be slapping on the cuffs.

"Are you aware that it's a felony to remove property from a bankruptcy estate?" the other agent said. "One count for each item removed."

I looked the agents in the eye. I wanted to let them know that their tactics didn't scare me, but it wouldn't have been the truth. A year's worth of loyalty to Charlie had built a sheen of invincibility around me; but Charlie was out in California, his watch and wallet and car keys stored in a manila envelope somewhere in the L.A. County court system. Upstairs, the newly installed trustee was surveying the landscape for the government. A survey of my own situation was grim: I was a college student in name only, having ditched my academics to throw my lot in with a boss who had gone to prison and likely wasn't coming back, possibly facing jail time myself.

I told them what they wanted to know. Teddy had failed to mention the cache of furniture on Charlie's property, and I drew them a detailed map, providing them with the gate code. "It's Charlie's wedding anniversary," I said nervously. The agents smirked, as if Charlie had no business even getting married.

"We'll be in touch," the agents said as the interview ended, which I hoped was just something they learned to say from watching too many movies about FBI agents, but they were, in fact, in touch a few days later, during dinner with my parents.

"It's the FBI," my mother said. "They want to talk to you."

I'd failed to mention my interview with the agents to my family or friends, mostly because I did not want their long-standing prediction that my employment at ACC would land me in prison to be validated. I took up the phone. An agent who was not one of the agents present at my interview breathed into the phone that based on my testimony they had cause to search Charlie's property, but they had mislaid the gate code. I repeated it from memory and hung up, then rejoined the dinner table, filling my family in on what was happening at work.

The next morning, those few Keating loyalists who remained were incensed about the invasion of Charlie's property.

"Someone sold out," a loyalist said, his voice riddled with accusation. He'd cornered me in a deserted hall in accounting.

"It's unbelievable," I said.

I was unfazed by the confrontation, though, knowing that the Keating loyalists would make a last stand and then fold, which they did quietly, one by one, submitting their resignations to the group that the trustee had put together to help govern what was left of American Continental, a group that included WSR, with whom I managed to get an audience when I learned that Teddy had made his exit plans: He was moving back to Chicago, a sure sign that the sea change at ACC was complete.

"We'll only be able to keep one runner," WSR said, explaining that because of ACC's enormous debts, the government wanted a skeleton payroll. I lobbied hard to be that one runner and won the position handily, the other runners preferring not to stay on to work for the trustee. As for me, loyalty to Charlie was no longer a luxury I could afford. I ditched the i like charlie keating button and helped with ACC's move from the roomy offices on Camelback Road to a smaller office in a building down the street, agreeing to answer the phones so that the full-time receptionist could be let go.

Fitzgerald Alive and Well in New York

I opened the Arizona Republic to a full-page photo of the author Bret Easton Ellis, sitting backward in a folding chair in what looked like someone's kitchen, on the front page of the Arts section. I stared dumbly at the picture, recalling the name from a midnight viewing of the film of his novel *Less Than Zero* years before. I'd been riveted by the portrayal of friendship flickering on the screen that night against the Southern California landscape and had hoped I was as reliable a friend as the protagonist. I'd noted that the movie was based on a novel and had been startled to discover that it had been written by a college student, which I read as a sign of sorts about my own ambitions to write, which resurfaced in the wake of the implosion of my relationship with Jenny.

Just as startling as seeing the photograph of Ellis was the attendant article about the furor caused by the recent publication of his third novel, *American Psycho*. The elements of the furor seemed fantastic: sections of the book being leaked to *Time* magazine by staffers at Ellis's publisher who abhorred the book; a boycott instituted by the National Organization for Women because of the graphic nature of the murder and torture committed by Patrick Bateman, the narrator of *American Psycho*, against women (forcing Ellis to travel with bodyguards, if he traveled); the last-minute pulping of the book by the publisher, who allegedly bent to the will of its parent company, Gulf and Western; the book being snapped up by another publisher (and Ellis being paid twice for the same book, him getting to keep the original six-figure advance). I gulped back the information, reading and rereading the article, the details weaving themselves into my personal fabric. For days after, the scandal was all I could think about. I was outraged at the First Amendment infringement by his original publisher, of course, but that Ellis's work was being boycotted (and consequently his life threatened) seemed impossible. And deliciously exciting. Not since *The Satanic Verses* had another book made an impression on the culture the way *American Psycho* had.

Ellis seemed to share much in common with F. Scott Fitzgerald. In the days before Internet searches, it was hard to come by the kind of biographical information that is so readily indexed and available in the modern age. The public library became the repository of all my spare time as I searched newspaper and magazine indices for the mention of Ellis's name. Reviews were aplenty, but only a shadowy sketch of the author's life was possible: I learned that, much like Fitzgerald, Ellis was the product of a private education; both had success at a young age (Fitzgerald was twenty-three when his first novel, *This Side of Paradise*, was published in 1920; Ellis was twenty-one when *Less Than Zero* was published in 1985); and both had written a first novel that scandalized a generation. There was certainly room enough in my infatuation with F. Scott Fitzgerald for his modern-day counterpart.

I was hungry to read more—anything more—by Ellis and quickly devoured his second novel, *The Rules of Attraction*, which was published the same year the film version of *Less Than Zero* premiered. Knowing that Ellis had recently graduated from Bennington College in Vermont made *Rules*, a multiple-narrator tale set at Camden College (a thinly fictionalized Bennington), an interesting read. I imagined Ellis revolving in the same world as Lauren and Paul and Sean, the myth about what it must be like to attend Bennington growing large in my mind. I imagined Dressed to Get Screwed parties spilling out of the common rooms of the clapboard dorms lining both sides of Commons Lawn, ending in free-for-alls at the End of the World; I imagined dorms littered with debris from the last, great can't-miss party; I imagined classmates who lived as if they were rock stars constantly on tour. The lack of biographical material overwhelmed my common sense about reading too much into an author's work. Plus, if *This Side of Paradise* was based on Fitzgerald's experiences at Princeton, who was to say *Rules* wasn't informed by Ellis's experiences at Bennington?

·

My infatuation with Bret Easton Ellis and *American Psycho* led me to apply to transfer from Arizona State University to Bennington College. I spent countless hours staring at the photo of what I later learned was the Commons, imagining myself ensconced in the woods of Vermont, pecking away at a brilliant manuscript. Bennington's outrageous tuition—then the most expensive college in the country—or how I would pay for it, didn't faze me. I was willing to borrow it without the hope of ever paying it back, if necessary. I filled out the application in a fever, pressing my current teachers for recommendations. Upon receiving my application, Bennington called to inquire if I was available for an interview. I reluctantly admitted that a trip to Vermont for an interview was cost prohibitive. No matter, was Bennington's reply; they could arrange for an interview with a local alum in my area. I was given the name of a graduate who was now a practicing physician in downtown Phoenix, with instructions to contact her to set up the interview.

My application languished as I fingered the note I'd made with the alum's information, the paper rife with creases from folding it inside my wallet with the intention of calling from work, full of holes from repinning it to the wall in my bedroom. My daily proximity to lawyers had revived the idea of attending law school, and the pull to make money was a force that overpowered the idea of spending tens of thousands of dollars to attend a school that didn't even give grades. Still, the lure of writing a book that would contribute to modern culture in the way that Bret Easton Ellis had appealed to me. But it was a gamble, and while I wasn't averse to risk, I wanted the risk to be calculated.

•

Charlie Keating was convicted of seventeen counts of fraud, racketeering, and conspiracy and sentenced by California superior court judge Lance Ito to the maximum, ten years, which Charlie would serve at a medium-security federal correctional institution in Tucson.

•

As the dismantling of Charlie's empire reached its final stages, I found myself apprenticed to WSR—the lawyer that the government's trustee had charged with all legal matters relating to the bankruptcy of American Continental—as a Boy Friday, eventually working out of his Paradise Valley mansion, where he'd set up his office, replete with two secretaries that had followed him over from American Continental. The four of us were a machine whose function was the dissolution of everything Charlie had spent his career building.

I reveled in my position as WSR's lieutenant and enjoyed a number of perks and privileges that came with the position, namely the use of his house and cars while he was away on frequent business trips. It was easy to slip into the notion of Jay Gatsby, roaming the spacious mansion, traipsing from room to room, anxious to know if one day I'd live the kind of life I fantasized about. It was hard to know either way.

•

My dream of attending Bennington still burned, but it drifted into the category of Things Likely Left Unrealized. The internal compromise came in the form of my transferring to the

University of Arizona, in Tucson, a hundred or so miles south of Phoenix. Remnants of the heyday of U of A's creative program were still in place, and the two years there would be a proving ground to see if the writing life was for me. So without knowing a soul, I picked up and moved to an unfurnished apartment (which remained unfurnished save for a bed, a desk, and a radio) right off Speedway, the main thoroughfare near the university. With no telephone, television, car, or job, I would be able to spend every extra minute writing the novel that would be my calling card into the world of letters.

The Vegetable (King)

Without a car, I began haunting campus to kill time, the fourth floor of the Modern Languages Building on the palm-tree-studded lawn in the heart of campus in particular. I flipped through the listings of contests posted on the department bulletin board, admired the display of dust jackets of the books published by graduates and faculty, and became a familiar face to the faculty, whose tiny offices were overflowing with great books. Having transferred at the beginning of the calendar year, I felt like I was jumping aboard a ship that had set sail from a previous port: Those students who had entered the program together seemed to know one another and had a working knowledge of one another's artistic intentions, though it was easy to assimilate into this community once I exhibited a commitment to the common goal. The sense of certain failure at what we were all trying to accomplish—i.e., to live the writing life—bonded us tightly together.

My continual rereading of *American Psycho* convinced me that the highly pornographic imagery in the novel contributed heavily to the outrage about the book, and I decided to take up this fight in my own work. The idea that a reader's prudishness could be used against a work of art was highly offensive, and I knew the only way to exorcise these conservative demons from the reading public was to continue to treat pornography as an essential element of literature. I set about writing a novel called *The Vegetable King*—the title an homage to Fitzgerald's failed play, *The Vegetable*—along these lines, imbuing the narrator with the same general qualities as Patrick Bateman, the narrator in *American Psycho*. I carefully studied the ways in which Ellis wove the fabric of Patrick Bateman's personality, and set out to duplicate this texturing, to ensure that the pornographic scenes would be believable. I knew the scenes could be dismissed as gratuitous if the groundwork wasn't laid, and it wasn't my intention to titillate or to scandalize; I simply wanted a serious discussion of how pornography was a viable element of literature.

I wasn't to be satisfied in this, though, as my classmates talked around the pornographic scenes, the girls in my workshop viewing me askance as they waited their turn to discuss what I'd handed in. That a young, single, college-aged male who lived alone in an apartment without furnishings, a television, or a telephone was writing pornography was, in hindsight, probably not a surprise to anyone in my workshop, and it quickly became clear that an honest discussion about the use of pornography was not forthcoming. A few brave souls piped up to say they thought the pornographic scenes were extraneous and distracting, an argument I easily dismissed in my mind as amateurish and conservative.

Another frustrating aspect of the workshop was that I was allowed only so many turns in the rotation; with no job and no social obligations, I was churning out twenty or so pages a week, and even when I did come up in the rotation, I couldn't reasonably expect my classmates to read much more than fifteen pages. I needed another audience, and so I floated the idea of starting an outside writing group among a few friends in the program, startled at the overwhelmingly positive reception. I quickly committed to the idea and hosted the first meeting at my spacious apartment, everyone sitting cross-legged along the bare walls. I christened the group the Burgundy Club in homage to Herman Melville, who founded the first Burgundy Club (which referred to him and a bottle of wine, alone at a table, when the other New York clubs wouldn't offer him membership), and the name was immediately ratified. Between workshops and the Burgundy Club, I was able to finish a complete draft of *The Vegetable King*, which I considered a finished draft.

The next step, of course, was finding a publisher. If I were to follow in Ellis's footsteps, my pedigree needed to mirror his as closely as possible, which meant publishing a novel while I was still in college. So I spent afternoons in the university library, researching publisher and agent addresses, stopping at the computer lab before and after each research trip to print out a chapter of my novel, since I did not have a printer of my own. The lab monitors were notoriously vigilant about students making multiple copies, so I developed a routine where I would hit each computer lab in a rotation that never allowed the same monitor to see me twice. Armed with a list of the top publishers, I dipped into my student loan money for a day at the post office, sending off as many copies as I was able to produce clandestinely.

By day two, the wait to hear back was so excruciating that

I had to manufacture reasons to leave the apartment, to occupy my mind with thoughts about something other than literary success. I took long walks around Tucson, sometimes hiking the levels of the university parking garage near my apartment to take in a panoramic view of the Old Pueblo. I spent evenings at the campus dollar cinema, one in a crowd of a dozen or so who were paying to see a movie they'd seen a thousand times before. Another time-wasting routine was to stand at the magazine rack at the campus bookstore and leaf through the glossies, passively reading interviews with celebrities or articles about celebrities or perusing photos of celebrities—anything that might distract me from the vision I kept having of my book face-out on a bookstore shelf, and then to distract me from the stream of rejections flowing from New York publishers who didn't want to publish *The Vegetable King*.

One particular evening I was golfing a tennis ball around my barren apartment, contemplating a rewrite of my manuscript, when the doorbell rang. I opened the door to find a UPS driver, a thick package under his arm. I spotted the Random House return label, my hand shaking as I signed for the package, and sensed that the venerable publisher was delivering me good news express. A classy act, sending me the news via UPS, I thought, knowing they had probably tried unsuccessfully to locate me via phone. I thought of the story of F. Scott Fitzgerald running up and down Summit Avenue in Saint Paul, stopping traffic, when he learned that Charles Scribner's Sons was going to publish his first novel, *This Side of Paradise*.

I ripped open the envelope, packing material falling around me like snow. I wondered if Random House had just gone ahead and sent me a contract, maybe even a check for a healthy advance on what was sure to be a lifetime of royalties. I dropped the copy of my manuscript on the floor to free up my hands to deal with the unsealed envelope bearing the same stamp as the return label. I read the letter slowly, realizing the words "not right for our list at the moment" were meant not just for me, but for anyone who had sent them an unsolicited manuscript.

A sickness enveloped me and I crawled into bed, skipping classes the following day.

•

I found a note addressed to me taped to the gate of my apartment complex from one of the editors at *Persona*, the undergraduate literary magazine, accepting a short story I had written about a polygamous Mormon, called "A House Divided." As I had no phone, the editor explained, she'd decided to leave the note, which I pinned to the wall of my barren apartment as a badge of my first published work. I wondered if Jenny would ever see a copy.

•

Another afternoon spent flipping through the clipboards full of writing contest flyers on the fourth floor of Modern Languages yielded the information that Bennington College was starting a low-residency MFA program where aspiring writers would meet on the Bennington campus for two weeks twice a year. Published writers would serve as mentors for the semesters between residencies. The photo of a desk lamp atop a wooden desk under the eaves of a clapboard house contributed to the excitement coursing through me.

I stole the poster so that no one else could apply.

•

I happened upon the latest issue of *Entertainment Weekly* at the grocery store, an issue that contained a scathing review of *The Informers,* a new book by Ellis. I read and reread the article, amazed that I'd heard nothing about this book (but then, how would I have?), picking through the venomous article to find out what the book was about. *The Informers* was, it seemed, a short story collection set primarily in Los Angeles—a return to Ellis's hunting ground. The review reignited a thirst for All Things Ellis, and I obsessed about what Ellis's life was like post–*American Psycho.* Did he still need bodyguards? Was NOW still out to get him? I put myself on the waiting list for the library copy of *The Informers*, hoping the book would answer these questions. While waiting to read Ellis's new book, I sated my appetite by writing a letter to the editor at *EW,* chastising the magazine for jumping on the anti-Ellis bandwagon, which they printed in an issue a couple of weeks later under the heading "Hip Stir":

Once again a reviewer has overlooked the technical and literary genius of one of the brightest authors of our time, Bret Easton Ellis, whose work does represent the state of hip fiction today. I'll wager Lisa Schwarzbaum thinks Douglas Coupland is hip.

—Jaime Clarke, Phoenix

•

I wondered if Bret had read my letter to *EW.* I hoped so. I wanted him to know that the People were behind him. I also wondered if Jenny had seen it, if she found it an interesting clue as to what I was up to. That Fitzgerald had chronicled his life in a ledger and kept a modest archive was never far from my mind. It was how his story lived on, I surmised, biographers following the trail he'd left. I was less concerned about posterity than I was Jenny, who our mutual friends had informed me had recently married her college sweetheart. As far removed as I was physically from Phoenix and everyone and everything I'd known, the news of Jenny's marriage steeled my will to continue to build a new life of my own.

•

A glimpse into Ellis's life finally came in the form of a profile in the August issue of *Vanity Fair.* I skipped lunch and shelled out for the cover price so I could peruse the article in private. At last, here was real information about my hero: He was living in Virginia with a friend, having had to escape New York to get any writing done. The article described Ellis as "bulky," which I guess surprised me, for reasons that I couldn't explain. (The article didn't include any photographs, though a full-page caricature emphasizing Ellis's cherubic features graced the page opposite the article.) The odd detail of Ellis picking up a bath towel off the floor and sniffing it to see if it was clean stayed with me longer than it should've.

I was so grateful for the profile that I fired off a letter to *Vanity Fair*, which they printed in a subsequent issue under the heading "Bret Noir":

Finally a quasi-revealing profile (as much as we'll ever know, I'll bet) of one of the most talented writers of our time. As a senior studying creative writing at the University of Arizona I can say that Mr. Ellis is among the most revered authors of my generation, admired for the fluidity of his prose style and his eye for context and detail, which, on the surface, appear ordinary enough but are really, under Mr. Ellis's microscope, threatening and truly unnerving. I quiver with anticipation for the arrival of his latest masterpiece.

—Jaime Clarke, Phoenix, Arizona

•

My creative writing teacher told me that "A Complete Gentleman," the short story that emerged from my failed novel, was probably publishable and encouraged me to send it out to literary magazines. So I spent a week making copies and an afternoon stuffing envelopes and licking stamps, buoyed by my teacher's words. A few months later, Chelsea, a literary magazine in New York, sent a penciled note to say they were accepting "A Complete Gentleman" for publication in an upcoming issue to be determined. I told everyone who would listen about my first nationally published story.

East Egg

That's me in the backseat of the Lincoln Town Car as it barreled through the Vermont snow. I'd dozed off after the driver picked me up at the Albany airport, where I'd spent the night curled up on an uncomfortable half bench, the strap of my duffel bag looped around my arm in the event that someone tried to rob me. Sleep came fitfully and then was banished forever with the whir of an industrial vacuum cleaner as the sole terminal was cleaned in the early hours. I cursed myself for purchasing the cheaper red-eye ticket, and for not realizing that my arrival time would imprison me at the airport until 6 a.m., the first available time the car service could give me. These rookie mistakes seemed obvious as I trudged in circles through the tiny airport, my eagerness to get to Bennington College having fueled my poor decision making. After dreaming of broaching its verdant lawns, I was only a few miles away.

The thought that the chauffeur could pull the Town Car to the side of the deserted road and rob me—or leave me for dead—grew proportionate to the length of time we rode without seeing any houses, or any other cars. The sun glinted off the fields of snow, and I shaded my eyes to take in the rural landscape. We passed through a red-planked covered bridge worn by time, the landscape replaced by the bridge lattice-work, the interior of the car spotted with sunshine. The Town Car shot through the other side of the bridge, delivering us among the town of Bennington, a picturesque New England hamlet populated with wide, snow-encrusted lawns running back toward quiet houses nestled far from the road. The driver nosed the car through the gates of Bennington College, itself set far away from the main road. An admixture of anxiety and excitement coursed through me as the car crept along College Drive, finally slowing to a stop in front of the Barn, the two-story structure that had once housed dairy cows and whose first floor functioned as the administration building. The driver let me off in the small circular driveway in front of the Barn, our breath streaming from our mouths and nostrils as we exchanged pleasantries and I paid the tip. I watched the black car drive away, a blight on the winter landscape until it turned the corner and disappeared, the curtain of snow and sun falling again over the still campus. The buildings looked deserted: the Commons ahead of me, Crossett Library to my left, Commons Lawn a quiet runway of ice and snow running toward the End of the World, the abrupt end of the lawn from which you could see endless miles of woods and Vermont sky.

The snowcapped Green Mountains in the distance were a stark contrast to the orange-and-pink sun that had enveloped me a month earlier as I lay poolside in a chaise lounge, worried about what I would do if I wasn't accepted into the low-residency MFA program at Bennington. I hadn't heard, and it was clear to me only then that I maybe should've applied to a few more places (or at least Iowa; everyone was applying to

Iowa). While I made no assumptions about being accepted into the Bennington program, I hadn't prepared for the idea that I wouldn't be, so a phone call a few days later from the director at Bennington notifying me of my admission was the equivalent of surfacing from a dive in the deep end: heart racing, gulping air, relieved to be able to breathe again.

The intermission between my acceptance and actually arriving at Bennington—graduation, saying good-bye to friends in Tucson, scouring stores in Phoenix for winter clothing, buying a plane ticket—was a blur, the single thought that I was going to be a student at Bennington College, Bret Easton Ellis's alma mater, too unreal to believe; and I realized only as I stomped through the Vermont snow, waiting for the dorms to be opened, that I knew very little about Ellis's existence on campus. I wondered which of the green-and-white clapboard dorms he'd lived in. McCullough? Booth? Canfield? I set my bag down on one of the picnic tables outside of the Commons and scanned the lawn for any sign of life. I was eager to commune with like-minded writers, sure that we'd all come to study in Ellis's shadow. Bret Easton Ellis probably sat at this picnic table, I thought. He probably partied in this dorm, I thought as I was finally let into my room. He probably stared out this window, I thought as I looked again for signs of life on campus. He may even have lived in this very room, I thought as I drifted off to sleep, exhaustion washing over my body as I lay fully clothed on top of the bed.

A sound like a child banging a spoon on an overturned pot forced me awake, panic-stricken. My eyes adjusted to the dim light as my brain struggled to figure out where I was. The clanking resumed, and I put my hand on the metal register, the heat warming my fingertips. Out my window I could see dark figures moving against the gray landscape, some struggling with overpacked bags, others darting in and out of their dorms, unpacking idling cars.

My fellow Benningtonites had finally arrived.

I hurriedly showered and dressed for the first official event of the residency, the five o'clock cocktail reception, which was filled with friendly faces eager to hear how I'd come to the program, offering up their own stories. I told them about Ellis and about how I'd tried to transfer to Bennington as an undergraduate, and was more than a little surprised that they hadn't heard anything about the brouhaha over *American Psycho*, didn't know who Bret Easton Ellis was. Perplexed, I casually polled those in my new peer group to see if they knew that Bernard Malamud, author of such classics as *The Natural*, *The Assistant*, and *The Fixer*, had taught for more than twenty years at Bennington, a fact I'd learned with a little research, dropping this tidbit into conversation. But Bennington's history seemed to be just that.

Bennington's recent history was very much on everyone's minds. Just a year earlier, the college had taken the extraordinary step of abolishing tenure, firing twenty-six of the seventy-nine professors who taught at Bennington, invoking the ire (and censure) of the American Association of University Professors. Bennington claimed the abolition of tenure as a step in a vigorous restructuring program, one that would elevate the academic atmosphere; but all anyone wanted to talk about was the fact that Bennington College might close its doors before we graduated from the low-residency program. That the outcome and legitimacy of our situation was predicated on actions taken by the college during the academic year helped to plant the idea that those of us in the low-residency program were somehow second-class citizens, or at the very least outsiders to the college, an idea that was solidified in my mind when I strolled into the alumni office on the first business day of the residency.

"I'm a student here and would like the address for an alum," I said to the girl on the other side of the counter.

"You're a student here now?" the girl asked suspiciously.

I assured her I was, not realizing that the undergraduates enjoyed something called Field Work Term, where students left campus and chased their passions in the real world, so that once they cleared out at Christmas, they weren't back on campus until March. "I'm in the MFA program," I added.

"Oh." Her face went flat. She called out to an unseen woman in the office behind the counter. "Do the MFA students have the same privileges as the regular students?"

A rising nervousness pulsed through me. I was angered less by the condescension in the girl's voice than by the fact that somewhere in this tiny room was a file with Ellis's address on it, the key to contacting him directly. The girl disappeared into the office behind her, and I shifted my feet, trying to seem relaxed, as if I weren't worried about whether or not I would get what I had come for and were in no hurry to receive it. I tried to subvert my nervous tendency to assume that I could be outed as a fraud at any moment, and to replace it with the air of expectation that only the truly privileged can pull off successfully.

"Here you are," the girl said, handing me a yellow Post-it note, an address in New York City scrawled in her childlike handwriting. I memorized the address immediately, in case something disastrous happened to the Post-it, and then folded the information into my pocket. Ellis's address in hand, I jogged to Crossett Library, opposite the Barn, and asked the librarian for access to Bret's thesis. I noted the title, "This Year's Model," when the librarian handed it to me. Ellis's penchant for naming his work after the work of Elvis Costello felt like the first real clue to his personality. I secreted myself away in the basement with the manuscript, a collection of short stories, relishing my status as one of the few who had access to more work by Bret.

After reading the stories front to back, I carefully returned the manuscript to the librarian, falling in with a crowd headed for a lecture by President Coleman, who told us emphatically that Bennington College was not closing its doors and that we should clear our minds of this possibility and pursue our graduate work with the college's assurance that our degrees would be worth the work we put into them.

I recognized that others were putting more work into their degrees than I was.

The social aspect of life in the Bennington MFA program was too tempting; having stowed my personality away in an unfurnished apartment in Tucson—penance for wasting the first two years of college in Tempe, I thought—I was eager to have communion. My class being just the third admitted, the student body was a mere fifty or sixty strong, a number small enough that we could band together, hang out, and generally repair to our own good company.

The flight back to Phoenix after the first residency was akin to coming to periscope depth, and it took me a few days to readjust to life outside the residency. My sole determination was to revise *The Vegetable King* into a publishable manuscript, and I started feeding thirty pages a month to my mentor, eagerly awaiting his comments about how to revise the novel.

I tacked the Post-it with Bret Easton Ellis's address up on the wall in my study, a wall papered with the many rejection notices I'd received from the literary magazines I had inundated with the short stories I'd written in college, buoyed by my success in placing "A Complete Gentleman" with *Chelsea*. I intended to send Ellis a copy of "A Complete Gentleman," but when I returned from Bennington, a handwritten note from the magazine, indicating that my story had to be pushed back to a future issue because of spatial concerns, altered my plans. On the one hand, I imagined Ellis received dozens of manuscripts (both solicited and unsolicited) in the mail every day, and I didn't want to contribute to that slush pile; but on the other hand, I was eager to get on his radar. In my imagination, I'd like to believe that the struggle over the decision to wait for a copy of the published story versus sending a manuscript copy was an immense, intense fight, but in reality I probably knew the moment I learned of the story's delayed publication that I could not bear to stare at Ellis's address day after day without writing. And so I wrote a carefully worded letter—I didn't want to come off as too fawning, some sort of superfan who was to be feared—describing my admiration for Ellis's work and my current status as a Benningtonite and mailed it with a manuscript copy of my story to the address in New York. I also enclosed photocopies of my letters to the editors of *Entertainment Weekly* and *Vanity Fair* for good measure, to show I was a worthy acolyte.

The interim boredom in waiting for a response from Ellis—some days I reasoned that he wouldn't write back because of the sheer magnitude of correspondence he must have to deal with, other days I was sure the enclosure of my letters to both *Vanity Fair* and *Entertainment Weekly* signaled that I was some sort of lunatic—was vanquished by my monthly packets from my mentor, whose criticism of *The Vegetable King* remarkably mirrored the published criticism of Ellis's *American Psycho*. A couple of months into the mentorship, I wasn't able to view my manuscript as anything but a pale imitation of *American Psycho*, and I abandoned the book completely, boxing it and storing it in my closet, desperately trying to suppress the growing fear that *The Vegetable King* was a tangible product of my wanting to actually become Bret Easton Ellis rather than write a substantial novel of my own.

There wasn't time to ruminate on the nature of my admiration for Ellis, though, as I came home one night to find a typed, one-paragraph letter from Ellis thanking me for sending him my work, which he claimed to have read and enjoyed. I ran my fingers over the sentences, feeling the raised lettering, the letter having actually been typed on a typewriter. I studied the signature, a bulbous capital B followed by a smaller, tight script r-e-t. I reread the letter several times, convincing myself that Bret Easton Ellis was a fan of my work, Bret's stamp of approval a sure sign that "A Complete Gentleman" should be turned into a novel, an endeavor I started almost immediately after tacking Bret's letter up front and center on the wall above my desk.

•

In line at the Albertsons near my house, I perused the back page of Details magazine, reading a one-page article about a couple of girls calling themselves Shampoo. It was not immediately clear that Shampoo was a band, and I came away from the Q&A thinking the girls in Shampoo were explicitly and exclusively bidding to become celebrities for the sake of celebrity. The novelty of the idea seemed ingenious, and I scratched out a short story called "We're So Famous" in one sitting, imagining a fictional version of the idea featuring two talentless girls from Phoenix who simply desire fame.

•

My first summer residency at Bennington was marred by the fact that my first mentor, the writer assigned to read my monthly packets and correspond with me about them, had disappeared a month or so into our mentorship. I said nothing, unsure of what to do. When it came to light that he'd quit responding to all his mentees, we were hauled up to the faculty house where the director lived, one by one, and questioned. The problem of the Disappearing Mentor was made out to be our problem, and we were informed we wouldn't be given credit for that first semester, a real dilemma, as I was on financial aid and wouldn't be eligible to borrow for an extra semester. Suddenly the entire enterprise seemed in jeopardy and I considered quitting, limiting my financial losses to the five thousand dollars paid for the first term. Distracted, I mentioned the drama to one of the other writers on staff, whom many of us admired for her outspokenness and her capacity to mother us when the situation called for it.

By lunch word reached me that we would be receiving credit for the first residency and that we'd simply be expected to do a little extra work during the second.

•

I entered my short story "We're So Famous" into a contest held by the literary magazine *Mississippi Review*, edited by Frederick Barthelme, a writer a lot of us admired, and while it didn't win, the story was a finalist, and I learned the story would be published along with the winner and other finalists, an honor I had no idea about when I entered the contest.

The City Seen for the First Time

That's me in front of the publishing house Simon & Schuster, the parent company of Fitzgerald's publisher, Scribner, and the publisher that canceled *American Psycho,* my friend N—— snapping a photo I knew I'd hang above my desk back in Phoenix as a reminder of my first foray into New York City. Over the course of the Bennington residencies, my friendship with N—— had grown to the point where she immediately invited me to stay with her when I told her I needed to go to New York. I lived for the biannual ten-day residencies at Bennington not just because they were a chance to see old friends (and make new ones), but because the residencies were a chance to break the work-write-sleep-eat-work-write-sleep-eat schedule I'd set for myself in order to churn out pages of my novel, which, by the start of my second full year in the program, had grown to somewhere in the neighborhood of a hundred manuscript pages, a respectable stack of paper I piled neatly in a tray on my desk, fanning through it whenever I felt my enthusiasm sag.

The residencies served another purpose, too, a reminder of how quickly time was passing. My second winter in Vermont,

I recalled how, when applying to the MFA program, I had thought the two and a half years an eternity, but faced now with just two more full residencies, I laughed at how little time the five-residency program really was. Adding to the sense of urgency was the fact that during my third residency the first class would be graduating and would have to deliver their student lectures, one of the main requirements for graduation, along with writing a twenty-page paper and turning in a finished manuscript. As our own graduations loomed, the second and third classes were extremely curious about the nature of these lectures, and the anxiety on the faces of the first class that winter revealed that they weren't too sure themselves what the program was looking for. Would the lectures be scholarly? Would they be personal? Could they be funny? Could we simply get up there and read our twenty-page papers?

We piled into Barn 1, a stuffy classroom in the admin building, to hear the first lecture, breath bated. The audience was standing room only, bodies huddled against the winter cold swirling outside the thinly paned Victorian windows. Someone cracked open the door in the back of the classroom that led directly outside, a wisp of breathable air circulating throughout the room. The first victim, a well-liked man in his forties, rose tentatively to the front of the room, shifting nervously as he fumbled for some opening remarks. The room exploded into applause, both for the lecturer's sake and for our own. We knew it wouldn't be long before we'd be looking for similar charity, and we clapped madly, finally settling into the first lecture of the fledgling Bennington MFA program, a lecture on the history of the linoleum book, an oddity the lecturer had discovered while rummaging through the remainder bins at his local bookshop. We listened intently, learning more than anyone ever would about how linoleum books were made, who was making them, and why. At the finish of the presentation, we stood on our feet, drowning the lecturer in applause, happy for him that he'd completed his requirements but also for us, the lecture having revealed to us that anything would go, a hypothesis that held as we heard the rest of the lectures from the first class, which ranged from the personal to the scholarly, inspiring the second and third classes to follow their lead.

My writing days back in Phoenix following the residency were divided between work on my novel A Complete Gentleman and worry about what my lecture should be about. I had some time to think it over, but I wanted the issue settled, and confided in my then mentor, the writer Amy Hempel, that I was less comfortable giving a straight topical lecture. She encouraged me to consider giving a personal lecture, telling about my creative journey. This welcome advice relieved me of the self-inflicted anxiety caused by scratching out a short list of possible lecture topics, vague notions related to literature or fiction that would have to be supplemented and substantiated with many passages from classic and contemporary novels, a task that depressed me beyond thought.

I began to think about a personal lecture, something that meant a great deal to me. During these deliberations, two copies of the published version of "A Complete Gentleman" arrived in my mailbox. I held the green-and-orange cover of the issue of Chelsea, marveling at my name in alphabetical array with other writers, some I'd heard of, some I hadn't. I peeked at my story, careful not to break the spine. Seeing my name printed above the title, the words I'd written so long ago set neatly in a pleasing font, was as satisfying as winning a Pulitzer, and the thought of the effort and sheer luck (and waiting) involved in the process that had resulted in my first publication was exhausting. And while I recognized that in the scheme of things, my first publication was a small step, it felt like a step into a new world, the world of the professional writer, and was therefore both an end to the always-rising feeling that the nights and weekends spent locked in my room were a foolish waste of time and the beginning of my hope that I would continue to improve so that I could live a life of letters.

In thinking about my extraordinary good fortune, I knew that my application and acceptance to the Bennington MFA program had played a central role, and I wondered at the small chance that had brought me to Bennington: the midnight showing of *Less Than Zero* I'd viewed in high school. And I wondered if my journey to Bennington would be of interest to my classmates. After all, wasn't the experience of writing (on both sides of the page) a journey? I turned the idea over, arguing for and against it, depending on the day or my mood. The ithought of giving a vanity lecture repulsed me—I knew I would never sit through one and therefore couldn't ask anyone else to—but was there room to articulate this writer's personal journey without indulging in sophomoric mythmaking?

My nervousness about appearing egocentric aided in my devising a litmus test: I'd write Bret and ask if I could submit a series of questions to him, which he would answer and I would incorporate into my lecture. I reasoned that because Bret was central to my story as it related to Bennington, I was justified in including it; and if my story was of no particular interest, maybe others would attend as fans of Bret's work. If Bret didn't write me back or said no, that was a sign that the lecture topic was ill-conceived.

Two days after mailing the letter off to Bret, I started brainstorming alternate lecture topics, sure that Bret was not going to respond. I'd settled on an idea about contemporary fiction, a discussion of my then-favorite writers—Walter Kirn, Mary Robison, Sandra Cisneros, Denis Johnson, Jeffrey Eugenides, etc.—the thesis of said discussion something about the charge of contemporary fiction (a weak theme, I knew, but one I hoped would automatically flesh itself out once I started rereading my favorite books), when I came home from my job at a family-run print shop to a message from my father.

"Someone named Bret called," he said.

I knew I didn't have any friends named Bret, but the possibility that Bret Easton Ellis would pick up the phone and call me was so unlikely that it took a moment for the fact to register. My father handed me the message, the name Bret written in his scrawl, a number with the area code 212 beneath it. I picked up the phone and dialed the number, steadying myself against the kitchen counter. An answering machine clicked on after the second ring. Relieved, I started leaving a message— who I was and that I was returning a call—when the phone clicked in my ear.

"Hello?" intoned the same deep voice from the answering machine message.

I dumbly repeated what I'd said in my message.

"I got your letter," Bret said, "and I think it's a great idea." A clattering in the background distracted him for a moment, a muffled conversation ensuing. "Sorry," he said. "We're making soup."

I tried to imagine Bret Easton Ellis making soup in his kitchen in his apartment in New York City, a million miles away from my own kitchen.

"Why not come to New York," Bret offered. "Then we can sit down with your questions."

It took everything I had to remain calm. "Sure," I answered, trying to sound offhanded, as if I were going to New York anyway, as if I were unfazed at the prospect of flying to New York to meet my idol. I told Bret I'd let him know after the arrangements were made, checking first to see if he was going to be out of New York for any stretch of time.

"Nope," he said. "Come anytime."

I sleepwalked through the following days, dreaming of my trip to New York. Eager as I was to go, however, I needed time to prepare the interview. Suddenly the measly dozen or so questions I had been prepared to type and mail to Bret were insufficient, would somehow be an insult, and I reread all of Bret's books to come up with substantive queries about craft. I also reread the handful of magazine articles and reviews I'd collected over the years to come up with cult-of-personality questions; but frankly, years of curiosity about Bret brought an imbalance of these sorts of queries, and I chose them carefully, weeding out the more egregious fanboy questions. By the fall, I was ready for the interview.

While the purpose of my first trip to New York was to interview Bret, I booked an entire week so that I could visit N——, who lived with her husband, an actor, in Astoria, Queens. I wouldn't let myself get excited about the trip, though, until the city was in sight. As my plane drifted up the Hudson River toward JFK, I marked the twin towers of the World Trade Center, the Empire State Building, the gleaming spire of the Chrysler Building, the enormous green sprawl of Central Park. I peered across the person next to me to see Yankee Stadium, the ballpark shortly vanishing, replaced by the blue gray of the Atlantic Ocean as the plane circled the airport in search of the runway.

Once on the ground, I wanted to see up close the landmarks I'd viewed from the air. Waltzing up and down Fifth Avenue with N—— as a guide, I was amazed at how everything appeared just as it did on television, as if it were a set. I leaned on the rail outside at Rockefeller Center; I stood under the neon sign advertising the Letterman show; I dined in tiny, dark restaurants, the tables so close you could hear the conversation next to you.

I scoped out Bret's apartment, too, a day in advance of our interview, casually walking down the East Village street, careful not to stop and stare. The entrance was camouflaged with scaffolding, so I couldn't get a clear look at the face of the building, nor the address. I worried that it was the wrong building, a worry that caused a near psychotic break with reality as I rode in my first New York City cab, hurtling toward Bret and the interview, both a dream come true and a nervous nightmare.

The doorman under the green awning at the address I'd given the cabbie was on me right away, wanting to know whom I was there to see. I told him and he rang up.

"He'd like to know if you can wait a few minutes," the doorman said, not cupping the receiver. "He's not ready for you yet."

Iced out, I paced the marble floors of the lobby, the door-man never far from sight.

I flashed back over the last ten years of my attempts at writing, how I'd read Ellis's novels so many times my first writing was a clear appropriation, friends recognizing my rich, apathetic narrators from *Less Than Zero*, my page-long, comma-rich sentences creating the same rhythms as *The Rules of Attraction*, my deadpan pornography reading like choice passages from *American Psycho*. My admiration for Ellis's work had brought with it much curiosity about the author himself, my worship in the cult of personality unsated by the smattering of interviews over the years.

"Okay, you can go up," the doorman said.

The elevator lowered, then opened empty in the lobby. In the elevator, I was all nerves and fluorescent light; I stared at the cool metal of the narrow elevator, which moved soundlessly upward, stopping and opening all at once. In front of me, a cul-de-sac of doors stood closed in an elegant, dim light. I shuffled forward, squinting at the doors, trying to decide which was Bret's, when out of the corner of my eye I saw a door I hadn't noticed at first, cracked slightly, a cherub's face peeking Garbo-like out at me, grinning.

Becoming Jay Gatsby

I watched out the airplane window, marveling again at the toy city below. The months following my graduation from Bennington had left me without direction. The fact that I was the proud owner of a newly minted MFA had not interrupted or altered my life in Phoenix, where I lived at home and worked full-time. I continued to write, tinkering with the idea of writing my first published short story into a novel. I wrote a handful of short stories, too, sending them scattershot to various literary magazines around the country. As spring turned into another hot desert summer, I couldn't shake Bret's parting advice as we stood outside his building after the interview. "Have you ever thought about moving to New York?" he asked. I told him that the idea had never crossed my mind, not wanting to let on that I was floored that I was even visiting New York, the idea of actually moving to the city too big for me to comprehend. "It's a great place to be a writer," he said. "You should consider it." I forgot his advice as quickly as it had been offered, jumping into a cab and gaping at the buildings along Park Avenue as I made my way uptown to meet a friend. But his words revisited me as I struggled with what to do next.

I believed that if I could just get one book published, I would be able to establish some sort of career path that would allow me to make a living, however humble, and validate the time and effort and sacrifice I'd invested in the idea. Viewed this way, a move to New York seemed inevitable, and I was relieved at having the decision dictated to me in just that fashion.

I arrived in New York at the end of May with a thousand dollars in my pocket, the money I was able to save in the few weeks between my decision to move and the day my father dropped me off at Sky Harbor International. My Bennington friends in New York warned of the astronomical rents for city apartments, so I brought three times the amount of the most expensive apartment in Phoenix, knowing I would have to find a roommate situation to make it work, details that could be sorted out during the first two weeks of my visit, which I'd spend again on my friend N——'s couch.

I began my first morning in New York at my laptop, organizing scenes, sketching characters, tinkering with the outline for the novel. My attention was quickly derailed, though, the temptations of the city proving too enticing. By lunchtime, I found myself hopping the subway for Manhattan, wandering the streets for the rest of the day. Famous landmarks and addresses were my destination—the Empire State Building, MTV in Times Square, the New York Public Library, Central Park, Trump Tower. I stood staring up at the stenciling on the side of the former Charles Scribner's Sons building on Fifth Avenue, lamenting that the interior was no longer Scribner's offices, and that the ground floor, which was once one of the grandest bookstores in New York, was now a Benetton clothing store. I toured the lobby of the Plaza Hotel, poking my head into the dark-wood Oak Bar, imagining Fitzgerald at the bar, a martini in hand, or the anecdote about him and Zelda drunkenly splashing in the Plaza fountain, or riding on top of a cab out front. Soon I found myself accompanying N— into the city in the morning to spend my day in Manhattan, meeting her again to catch the subway home after five. Every morning offered a new opportunity for adventure against the backdrop of the city. I spent an entire day walking up one side of Fifth Avenue and down the other; I spent a day at the Museum of Modern Art, another at the Met; I milled around Chinatown and Little Italy; I rode the Staten Island ferry back and forth to see the Statue of Liberty.

Somewhere into the second week of my new life, I realized that I had spent more than half the money I'd saved for my move. My chances of finding an apartment dwindled as the days beat on, the meter running the minute I woke each morning. A dollar fifty for the subway. Ten dollars for lunch. Untold dollars for dinner and drinks with friends. Another dollar fifty for the subway home or, worse, twenty dollars for a cab ride after drinking too much to be able to ride the subway. I'd asked too much of my friends to be able to impose on them any longer, and I faced the real possibility of deportation back to Arizona. I researched cheap living arrangements—inquiring at the Y, pretending to be a New School student to access their roommate board—and found that there weren't any. My time in New York was quickly coming to an end, and I hadn't been gone longer than a few weeks. I was rescued from spending the last of my money on a one-way ticket to Phoenix by R——, a fellow Benningtonite, who lived in a farmhouse in Concord, Massachusetts, and who invited me to visit, offering her basement apartment until I could figure out my next move. I graciously accepted the offer, boarding a Greyhound bus for Boston, temporarily saying good-bye to New York.

F. Scott Fitzgerald Is
in the Conference Room

That's me in the conference room of Harold Ober Associates, the oldest literary agency in the country, reading the bound photostatic copies of the various handwritten drafts of *The Great Gatsby*, marveling at the last-minute addition of words and phrases that would come to mark the book's genius. I'd accepted the position at Ober the moment it was offered to me, canceling the other interviews I'd scheduled at the handful of literary agencies that had responded to the mass faxing of my resume, my sole plan for retaking Manhattan. I'd hatched the plan in my bunker in Concord, though the faxing took place at the family print shop back in Phoenix. My old manager had flown me back to work while he took a vacation, reasoning it was cheaper than hiring a temp. While in Phoenix, I had lunch with my old mentor, WSR, who was amused by my tale of bouncing from New York to Boston and back to Phoenix. At the end of lunch, he wrote me a check for enough money to get me back to New York, with the caveat that I would pay him back out of the advance for my first published book. I accepted under those terms, grateful for WSR's belief in what surely seemed like a hopeless scheme.

And while a carousel of sublets awaited, my new job was the organizing principle that distracted me from the truth about my living situation.

Walking into Ober's offices in midtown Manhattan was like climbing through a wormhole: Overhead lighting was eschewed for desk lamps, the ceiling tiles were yellow with cigarette smoke, and the drinks cart would make an appearance on Friday afternoons (except in the summer, when Fridays were half days). The office was also alive with the clattering of typewriters—typing was a prerequisite of the job, and my boss was somehow surprised that I had taken typing in high school and could center words on a page without the aid of a computer. Ober had computers, but the Internet was available only on a common terminal in the middle of the office, which made checking your personal e-mail an open declaration that you weren't, in fact, working when you should be. All Ober correspondence was dictated into Dictaphones, and I became expert at working the foot pedal—left to rewind, right to fast-forward, my boss's voice in my ears with the day's business.

Access to Fitzgeraldiana was not the only benefit of working as a lowly paid administrative assistant to the president: The Ober shelves abounded with the authors represented by the agency since its founding in 1929 by Harold Ober, then a junior agent at the Paul Reynolds Literary Agency, itself founded in 1893 by that agency's namesake, the first literary agent in America, whose clients included Robert Benchley, Erskine Caldwell, Willa Cather, Winston Churchill, Theodore Dreiser, Erle Stanley Gardner, Jack London, Norman Mailer, Malcolm X, W. Somerset Maugham, George Bernard Shaw,

Upton Sinclair, Wallace Stegner, Booth Tarkington, Thornton Wilder, and others.

The Ober client list was equally if not more impressive. Harold Ober left the Reynolds agency with just five clients: Fitzgerald, Walter D. Edmonds, Ezra Bowen, Catherine Bowen, and Thomas Beer. Unbelievably, Ober's interest in Fitzgerald was primarily for his short stories, which Ober was able to sell to the magazines of the day. Celebrated periodicals like the Saturday Evening Post and Collier's would pay top dollar for a Fitzgerald short story, and Fitzgerald famously gave of himself to create these popular fictions in order to have money to buy time to write novels, Fitzgerald's true ambition being to write a Great American Novel. The creative gulf between the short stories he wrote as entertainments and his serious literary novels was marked by the fact that while Ober handled the submissions of his short stories to magazines, Fitzgerald dealt directly with Max Perkins, his editor at Charles Scribner's Sons, when it came to selling his novels, an unwritten policy that would evolve as Ober developed its client list to include Chinua Achebe, Sherwood Anderson, Judy Blume, Pearl S. Buck, James M. Cain, Agatha Christie, William Faulkner, John Hawkes, Langston Hughes, Dean Koontz, Ira Levin, James Lord, Joseph Mitchell, J. D. Salinger, Dylan Thomas, and Glenway Wescott, among others. The Ober list contained some interesting oddities, too, like politicos Adlai Stevenson and Dean Acheson; Arnold Gingrich, founder of Esquire magazine; the actress Shirley MacLaine; Whitfield Cook, who wrote the screenplay for Alfred Hitchcock's *Stranger on a Train*; and David S. Lifton, whose book about the Kennedy assassination, *Best Evidence*, made me a lifelong believer in conspiracies. The Ober agency had also tried to sell *Casino Royale*, the first novel by Ian Fleming to feature the character James Bond, but no publisher was interested.

While my job at Ober was little more than clerical—sorting and distributing the afternoon mail, opening and stamping mail for my boss, answering the switchboard while the receptionist was at lunch, transcribing my boss's daily dictation, answering permissions requests to reprint Ober material for classroom use, filing, etc.—the names and titles of books I loved or at least had heard of added a measure of intangible glamour to the position. Too, my employment with Ober offered me an inside glance at the publishing game. I wrapped each of our clients' manuscripts as if it were a book I'd written, anxious to hear back from the editor we sent it to, disappointed when the manuscript was returned via courier with a declining letter, exuberant when a book was sold for publication.

Standing so close to the magical stream that took an author's work and made it accessible to the reading public inspired me to finish my own novel. I looked forward to the end of the day, when I would deposit the mailbag with the mail truck parked down on the street, grab some Chinese food, and head back up to the tenth floor, the Ober offices quiet except for the cleaning lady. I'd switch on the lights in the conference room and try to summon the ghosts of those writers from days gone by who had passed through the conference room when it was Harold Ober's office. Mostly I would wander the halls, pulling dusty books off shelves and answering the occasional phone call, since Ober didn't believe in the too-modern invention of voice mail. Other times I would stare up at the portrait of Dorothy Olding, the recently deceased matriarch of Ober. Olding had worked for Harold Ober and had succeeded him as proprietor when Ober died suddenly of a heart attack in 1959. By all accounts a no-nonsense woman, Olding had piloted the agency through its post-Fitzgerald golden years, even working from her apartment when she was bedridden with the effects of stroke until her death shortly before my employment.

One of my first assignments at Ober was to help clear out Ms. Olding's East Side apartment. My boss, the new president, had been named executor of the Olding estate, and I helped transport certain items—books, furniture, etc.—that had been left to the Ober offices. As I walked through the nicely appointed apartment, I imagined hundreds of late-night literary conversations turning to gossip, the thousands and thousands of manuscript pages read from aspiring writers. I marveled, too, at Ms. Olding's ability to transcend the politics of her time and rise to the top of the country's oldest literary agency. I lamented that another of the dwindling links to Harold Ober himself—and by extension Fitzgerald—had passed, ruminating on the fast-fading glory of a yesteryear I could only romanticize, a romance that lent a certain urgency to a spur-of-the-moment idea to interview Walter D. Edmonds, one of the original Ober clients. Coincidentally, Mr. Edmonds lived in Concord, Massachusetts, my old stomping grounds, and I quickly made contact with his daughter about my idea.

"He's quite ill," the daughter informed me.

I promised to be patient—and brief, if necessary—and the daughter relented. We agreed on a date, and I thanked her and hung up.

On the train ride to Boston, I fantasized about what personal memories Edmonds would offer about Fitzgerald, maybe a story about how they had taken lunch together around the corner from the Ober offices, or about Fitzgerald barging in on a meeting between Ober and Edmonds, full of himself and radiating glorious success. I craved to know something left out of the biography created over the fifty-some years since Fitzgerald's sad death in Hollywood, something to replace the image of Fitzgerald sitting in a chair in a bright room, poring over the Princeton football schedule while eating a chocolate bar, standing suddenly, grasping for the mantel, slumping to the floor as his great big heart gave out.

I called Edmonds's daughter upon arrival in Boston, apologizing for the lateness of the hour but wanting to confirm the interview.

"We thought you were coming last Saturday," the daughter said.

I assured her I had the right date.

"He was looking forward to talking to you," she said, "but he's too sick now. It's not possible."

I apologized repeatedly, the image of her sickly father anxiously awaiting my visit, then succumbing to confusion when I didn't show, making me sick to my stomach.

"He's too sick," the daughter repeated.

I asked if I could call in the morning to see if he was feeling better, and the daughter grudgingly agreed. When my call that Saturday went unanswered, I took it as a sign of the daughter's anger, not knowing until I reached the Ober offices the following Monday that Edmonds had passed away that Saturday, taking with him all that he wanted to tell me.

Edmonds's passing prodded me to continue with my fledgling idea for a history of Harold Ober. My bid to preserve the agency's past wasn't altruistic; I desired a small place in the story, if only as storyteller. And if I was to tell the story religiously, I would have to visit the shrine, the Ober archives housed along with the Fitzgerald archives at the Firestone Library at Princeton. My boss agreed to let me train to Princeton on Fridays, her reading day (which meant she wasn't in the office), and set up my clearance with the librarian at Firestone. And in a stroke of serendipity, my old college friend and fellow Fitzgerald fanatic H—— now lived in Princeton and could provide a couch for my visits.

On the train to Princeton, I fancied that I was dressed in tweed, reporting for the new school year from my hometown, envisioning it a cold and snowy hometown like Fitzgerald's Saint Paul, the steam of my breath recycling like the wheels on the locomotive bearing me toward the tree-lined comfort of Princeton. Before presenting myself to the archivist at Firestone, I walked the campus from one end to the other, strolling the quad, passing students roughly my age, wondering if they mistook me for one of their own. I stood in front of the house where Fitzgerald had lived on Prospect Avenue; I visited the subterranean bookstore; I hunted Fitzgerald's ghost in every stone corner. Finally I settled into a chair at a table in the library and summoned the first box of the Ober archives, gingerly flipping through files of yellowed typewritten letters surprising in their lack of detail about Ober the man, letters devoid of gossip or news of the day. My hope of preserving a romantic history fluttered away as I combed through the boxes, and I canceled the weekly train trips a few weeks into the project.

I Hear You're Looking for a Gonnection

That's me at a table at the Bowery Bar, the chic New York bar and grill built on the ashes of a defunct gas station, with Bret Easton Ellis, trying not to appear nervous. The writers David Lawrence and Jeff Gomez were seated around the table too, and I took my conversational cues from them. Lawrence, a classmate of Bret's from Bennington, mentioned something about the college, and I added a story of my own about my time at Bennington. Gomez mentioned something about his book, and I pretended to have read it and liked it. Sooner or later the talk turned to me—Lawrence and Gomez were probably wondering what the hell I was doing at the table—and Bret mentioned my unpublished novel, *A Complete Gentleman*, which he knew intimately, having graciously read and line edited three or four drafts. Bret called my book "interesting," and I felt like I'd just won the Pulitzer Prize for Literature.

I'd called Bret right when I moved to the city, telling him I'd taken his parting advice to move to New York after we met the previous year for the interview. His advice had led me to fantasize about being swept up in Bret's world, a fantasy that was fulfilled when I found myself at the Bowery

Bar; or at KGB, a bar on the Lower East Side, with Bret and Jay McInerney, attending a book party for Joshua Miller, the young actor from *River's Edge* who had turned author; or at dinner with Bret at Flamingo East, a swank bar and restaurant in Bret's neighborhood; or having drinks at a bar in the East Village before Bret headed uptown for a dinner with the legendary writer Joan Didion; or at Bret's annual Christmas party, chatting up the actress Parker Posey, whom I'd initially mistaken for a college student.

While the glitter of Bret's world was enticing, the real value of Bret's friendship was his unbelievable generosity with respect to my work. His patience and commitment to helping young writers was astounding. With Bret's help, I was able to finish a draft of *A Complete Gentleman* that I felt confident in, attracting an agent from the very literary agency where I worked, who began offering it to publishers around New York. The fact that I finally had a manuscript being read by editors put a skip in my step, and I indulged in the New York lit scene, redistributing my writing time to run around the city attending readings and book parties with or without invitation. The Sunday-night fiction reading series at KGB was the anchor to whatever the week held, the readings oftentimes the beginning of a night that would end well after midnight. My then roommate and fellow Benningtonite David Ryan would often accompany me on these sojourns, and we became friendly with the owner of KGB, as well as the coordinator of the reading series, who gamely asked David and me if we'd like to read in the series. The coordinator had a Sunday he couldn't book and we readily agreed. Our reading was the decided undercard on the schedule of readings that fall, but the reading got an unexpected boost from a reporter from the *New York Times*, who caught David and me at the bar after another packed Sunday-night reading. We chatted with the reporter, who seemed to be interviewing everyone in the place, and thought nothing of it until I received a phone call at work from Bret.

"You're in the *Times*," he said.

I bolted from my desk at Ober to the deli across Madison Avenue and bought a copy, then thumbed through the paper, discarding the unread sections into the trash, until I found the article titled "A Cold War Relic Is a Literary Hot Spot; New Authors Hope Someone Important Is Listening to Them at Bar's Readings." I scanned the piece, my eyes lighting on my name mixed in with the surnames of writers well-known and famous, the article a stroke of good fortune for an unknown trying to carve out a small corner of literature for himself.

And what was the probability that Jenny read the *Times?* Was it outrageous to fantasize about her coming across the article? Was she even aware of my move from Phoenix to New York? Everything pointed to her having no interest in me and my life, but it was too painful to consider that she wouldn't be interested, and I refused to believe it.

•

The calendar turned to October, and I ran out of couches and connections to places to sleep, so I moved my meager possessions into the Ober offices on Madison Avenue. The hardest part about living at the Ober offices was fooling the twenty-four-hour doormen, whom I simply befriended rather than insult. They looked the other way when I sneaked a bag of laundry out of the building, or when I ducked out early in the morning to grab a shower at the health club I'd joined on a trial membership for just that purpose, pretending to arrive to work with the rest of my colleagues.

I found my boss's office floor the most comfortable, owing to the padding under the rug.

•

"Lindy," a short story I wrote after reading an excerpt of the A. Scott Berg biography of the aviator Charles A. Lindbergh in a copy of *Vanity Fair* while watching the Ober phones at lunch, was accepted for publication by *Mississippi Review*. The story was published alongside a story by David Ryan, a happy coincidence. We arranged for a *Mississippi Review* night in the KGB reading series on the Lower East Side and gave away free copies of the literary magazine.

Montenegro

The New York press was seemingly fascinated with literary magazines. The legendary *Paris Review,* edited by George Plimpton, of course, but also a handful of start-ups: *McSweeney's, Fence,* and *Tin House.*

After some serious deliberations, David Ryan and I decided to join the fray. We went about researching how literary magazines operated. We used what contacts we had—Frederick Barthelme at *Mississippi Review* and Askold Melnyczuk at *AGNI*—and lobbed question after question. We learned about the dilemma of distribution, we learned about subscription drives and the importance of databases, we heard stories of production nightmares. We assembled a staff made up of friends from the Bennington MFA program and from New York. We knew we'd have the same mainstays that other literary magazines featured—fiction, nonfiction, and poetry. We decided to add a theater section; we wanted an art section, but we knew we couldn't afford to do it in color. Our art editor educated us about art that could be printed without color, and on regular stock rather than the glossy folio stock, which at that point might as well have cost a million dollars. We talked about the tricky classification of nonfiction. We wanted the nonfiction section to be creative nonfiction, but that left out a whole raft of nonfiction that was viable and relevant. We decided to add a criticism section, whose charge it was to publish social and cultural criticism, pieces not readily available in the slush pile but also not found in other literary magazines.

One of our fiction editors suggested the name *Post Road*, after the old mail route between New York and Boston, as our editors were split between the two cities. The magazine quickly became the perfect calling card for a group of young writers scurrying around New York trying to infiltrate the world of letters.

•

"What?" I said, looking up from my work. WS and CB, two Ober agents whom I also counted among my friends, stood grinning, WS fanning a piece of paper in her hand. Their grinning was infectious, and I started grinning too, though I had no idea why.

"Congratulations," they both said as WS handed over the sheet of paper.

My eyes scanned the faxed offer from Bloomsbury, the publisher that wanted to publish my novel *We're So Famous*, which I'd undertaken after every editor in New York declined to publish my first novel. Working nights and weekends, I'd been able to finish the book in a matter of months. I was sure that my agent would love *We're So Famous*, and was unprepared for the bad news that she didn't, in fact, love it and further let it be known that it wouldn't hurt her feelings if I looked for representation elsewhere. I thanked her—she was still a colleague of mine, and for the first time I realized how such a relationship could be uncomfortable—and wandered back to my desk, devastated.

I swore to myself I would do what I could on behalf of my little novel. I made a short list of the agents whose names I'd heard in passing during my time in publishing, flirting with the idea of trying to act as my own agent. I then made a smaller list of the assistants that I'd met in publishing. Working at a literary agency like Harold Ober didn't offer the same opportunities to mingle with your counterparts at other agencies the way working at a publishing house did. I'd made some connections through correspondence between my boss and someone else's boss, but these connections weren't personal, and so I was reluctant to send them my manuscript and ask them to champion it to their bosses.

Then I remembered my fellow Oberite OC's friend Panio, who worked at Crown, a division of Random House, one of the biggest publishers in New York, and whom I'd met on a night of drinking. OC was a good guy, but I'd been putting off his offer of a night on the town only because he ran with a younger crowd—he'd just graduated from NYU—and I worried about bringing down the age curve. But one night I accepted the proposition, and we headed downtown to Phebe's, a Lower East Side institution on the Bowery, across the street from the Bowery Bar and Grill. OC and I got a pitcher of beer and converged on a pool table, shooting stick and gossiping our way through the evening. Midway through our third game, Panio arrived, a good-looking kid with Hellenic features whom OC had known since grade school. Panio rotated in and out of our games, and the three of us chatted amiably, OC and Panio cracking each other up with jokes spoken in a code they must've developed back in their hometown in Massachusetts.

I wondered if Panio still worked at Crown—OC had long moved on from Ober to another job—and decided to send *We're So Famous* to him to see what he thought. I carefully packaged the manuscript and mixed it in with the other manuscripts going to Random House via the Ober messenger. The manuscript returned, quickly, though with a note from someone at Crown that Panio had moved to Talk Miramax Books, the new publishing company that functioned as an arm of the famous movie studio. I repackaged *We're So Famous* and had the Ober messenger deliver it to Talk Miramax. Again, the manuscript bounced back with a note informing me that Panio no longer worked at Talk Miramax. Discouraged by this chase, I decided to pursue finding an agent, knowing that having someone working on your behalf was the more prudent route, even though agents were notoriously reluctant to take on an unproven writer.

Over the course of shortening and lengthening my list of potential agents, Panio's name happened to pop up—he'd followed his boss at Crown to Bloomsbury USA, the American office of the London publishing house that had experienced an upswing in fortune when it published the Harry Potter books, and had become a full-fledged editor. This bit of news seemed serendipitous, and I fired a copy of *We're So Famous* over to Panio at Bloomsbury USA with a note reminding him who I was.

The days following Panio's receipt of the manuscript were agonizing; I imagined he was hungry for material and was in a good position to acquire novels for the new publishing house. But the days turned into weeks and months, and I finally gave up on hearing from him, too embarrassed to write him to find out if he'd read *We're So Famous*, knowing that he was probably dealing with professional writers who had professional agents, a sure sign that I should quit soliciting on my own behalf and find a good agent, which was my New Year's resolution when I returned from the holidays to an e-mail from Panio, who said he had good news for me.

I read and reread the cryptic e-mail, answering in as sanguine a tone as I could muster, barely containing my exuberance at the possibility that Bloomsbury USA might publish my book. I considered calling him, but I knew the excitement in my voice would give me away. Panio wrote back the same day to say that if I was interested in having *We're So Famous* published as a paperback original—meaning the book would not come out as a hardcover—Bloomsbury USA would like to publish my book. I said yes immediately, assuring Panio that I was not one of those writers who demanded his work be published in hardcover first. Panio was thrilled and sent a letter of extraordinary praise for *We're So Famous*, along with his plan to get me an offer in the next day or two.

Having come this close once before—an editor who read my first novel had called my agent and told her he was going to be making an offer, but when that offer didn't materialize, my agent called the editor only to be told he had taken a job at AOL—I kept the great news of my impending publication to myself, genuinely afraid of jinxing the prospect, an idea I kidded myself was ridiculous, until Panio seemed to disappear. From the tone of his e-mail, I'd expected an offer the following day, or at the very least before the weekend; but the weekend came and went without word. Not wanting to start our relationship off with me panicking about the offer, I busied myself at work, glad that I hadn't broadcasted the news to my colleagues at Ober. But they all knew once WS and CB handed me the faxed offer, which was accompanied by an e-mail from Panio begging forgiveness for the delay but that he'd been out sick for two weeks with the flu.

The sheer luck of Bloomsbury publishing *We're So Famous* made me a believer in chaos theory, or at the very least in the oft-repeated adage about the alignment of the stars and planets. The next step in the process was dealing with the contract department. Owing to the fact that Bloomsbury USA was still a small office equipped with mostly editorial personnel, the contract was issued from the London office, which would also be paying the advance out as prescribed by the offer sheet. As I had the resources of a full-fledged literary agency at my disposal, I forged ahead with negotiations, relying on WS or CB when I got stuck.

Shortly after signing the finally negotiated contract, Panio offered to take me to lunch to celebrate. We met for hanger steak at Les Halles, the Parisian brasserie on Park Avenue South near Panio's office. Proximity was not the only connection to Bloomsbury USA; the executive chef at Les Halles, Anthony Bourdain, was also a Bloomsbury author. Panio and I enjoyed our lunch in the noisy restaurant, gossiping about the publishing news of the day. He reiterated his earlier praise for my book, and I expressed my gratitude at his willingness to publish it. He walked me through the remaining steps in the process: The book would pass through copyediting, and I would receive the manuscript with any queries about style or content from the copy editor, Panio stressing that the queries were just suggestions and that I would have the final say; next would come the catalog copy, which Panio would write and show me, and which would most likely also be used on the back of the book's jacket; the final step would be to gather blurbs for the front and back covers. Panio asked me if I felt comfortable asking my published writer friends for blurbs, and I said that I didn't think it would be a problem to ask Bret Easton Ellis, who graciously provided a blurb:

> Jaime Clarke pulls off a sympathetic act of sustained male imagination: entering the minds of innocent teenage girls dreaming of fame. A glibly surreal world where the only thing wanted is notoriety and all you really desire leads to celebrity and where stardom is the only point of reference. What's new about this novel is how unconsciously casual the characters' drives are. This lust is as natural to them as being American—it's almost a birthright. Imagine Britney Spears narrating *The Day of the Locust* as a gentle fable and you'll get the idea.

I also asked Jonathan Ames, whom I'd met around town and whose book *I Pass Like Night* had inspired me to buy copies for everyone I knew one Christmas in college:

> Darkly and pinkly comic, this is the story of a trio of teenage American girls and their pursuit of the three

big M's of American life: music, movies and murder. This is an impressive debut by a talented young novelist.

The final quote came from Bob Shacochis, whom I'd met at Bennington. Bob was also overcommitted, it seemed, so I was especially moved when he took the time to read the novel:

Like a make-up artist, Jaime Clarke is a master illusionist; in his deft hands, emptiness seems full, teenage pathos appears sassy and charming. *We're So Famous* is a blithe, highly entertaining indictment of the permanent state of adolescence that trademarks our culture, a made-for-TV world where innocence is hardly a virtue, ambition barely a value system.

Hunting for blurbs was like begging for valentines, and I was only sorry when the process ran through, Panio saying three blurbs was more than enough for the book. Owing to various scheduling problems, *We're So Famous* would not be published until the spring of 2001, Panio assigning my thirtieth birthday as the official publication date, some nine months away, which seemed forever into the future.

There was nothing to do but wait.

Summit Avenue

That's me on the bus for the airport, leaving New York. As I sat staring out the bus window, I wondered if I'd be back and, if not, how much I'd miss the city that I'd loved the moment I first arrived. I'd intended to stay a few months longer, until my novel was published in the spring, but news that my apartment building in Williamsburg, Brooklyn—the first stable living situation I'd had since moving to New York—was to be gutted and renovated at the first of the year, turning me out on the street again, spurred my early return to Phoenix. Williamsburg had become something of a home to me too, as another fellow Benningtonite, Pete, one of my closest friends, lived down the street in his wife's childhood home, a three-story redbrick townhouse. I'd spent long afternoons on the stoop with Pete and his family, as well as his college friend and his family, who lived on various floors. The townhouse was the closest family I'd known since I left my own, and the blanket of comfort it had provided was essential to my staying in New York as long as I had. But I'd used everything I had or could borrow and had reached the bottom of what had seemed my limitless energy to make it in New York at all cost. And so I handed in my notice at Ober and stayed long enough to train my replacement.

I was a writer whose first novel was soon to be published, leaving the city I loved to move back home.

•

I wondered if Jenny knew anything about the fact that my novel was about to be published. I became acutely aware of how fruitless Gatsby's parties were, thrown in the hope that Daisy would saunter back into his life. Jenny had long ago ceased being a real person in my mind—she was of more use as an idea, one that had become too abstract to really grasp— and I couldn't summon a guess, or even remember the sound of her voice. Somewhere along the way, I'd lost all sense of her, though her presence in the world continued to pull on me.

The Middle West

That's me two years later on the houseboat, cruising Flathead Lake in Montana with my father and two brothers. We'd rented the two-thousand-square-foot lake house on Yellow Bay, near Bigfork, for our father's fiftieth birthday, though by the time my brothers and I could scrape together the necessary funds for the trip, our father was on his way to fifty-three. Regardless, we were excited about the trip and enjoyed the two-day drive from Phoenix through Utah and Idaho to the western corner of Montana, near Kalispell, our hometown. Spending the last couple of years back in Phoenix under the pretense of regrouping after life in New York had been a welcome circling of the wagons. My novel had been published, and I'd flown back to New York for the release party and for a reading at the Astor Place Barnes & Noble. My editor, Panio, showed up with a date, the actress Molly Ringwald, whom he would later marry. I was happy to have my novel in the world, tangible proof of my creative energies, and I was eager to write another novel, but moving back to New York seemed impossible and I couldn't guess what was next. I welcomed the reflection a trip to my hometown would bring.

As we made our way toward Montana through a June snowstorm, I wondered about what the word "hometown" meant to me. For most, the word evokes piety, or fondness, or something resembling a warm familiarity, but for me my hometown was frozen in time—it was always 1978 and I was always seven, my brother Jeremy only five, my youngest brother, Jared, never more than an infant; we lived in a redbrick house on Fifth Avenue West; my great-grandmother lived in a small green trailer across the street; my grandparents lived in a house a block away, my school, Elrod Elementary, on the next block over. Other memories—birthday parties, visits from cousins in nearby towns, sleepovers, Cub Scouts, swimming lessons at Woodland Park, skiing at Big Mountain in Whitefish, pitching for my Little League team—jockeyed for position, creating a crowded field of remembrances that seemed to span decades but in reality were crammed into a scant few years. When people asked where I was from, I answered with my hometown, a place whose topography is mostly in my head.

As we cruised the north end of Flathead Lake, the largest natural freshwater lake in the western United States, my father's hometown, Somers, came into view. My father's blue eyes flashed at the sight of the small town built on a hill by the Somers Lumber Company for the express purpose of creating a self-sustaining community for its workers, whose primary job was to create railroad ties for the Great Northern Railway. Somers was replete with a church, a school, a general store, a bank, and a post office with its own zip code. Over the course of the week, our father would take us on a tour of the Somers streets, pointing out the houses where his childhood friends had lived on the road that wound to the mansion at the top, where the bank president had lived. My brothers and I would see his childhood home, too, the garage he helped build with his grandfather, the small shed out back where he'd spent lazy summer nights, sometimes falling asleep to the sound of crickets and a transistor radio. "You'd still be living here if it wasn't for your mother," my father laughed, giving a nod to my mother's ambition to get away from small towns forever, an exodus we were all grateful for, though I wondered what it would've been like to grow up in Kalispell, to maintain the same friends my entire life, knowing something intimate about the landscape, sowing some patchwork into the fabric. As I listened to the narrative of my father's history—how the old train tracks were paved for a bike path he would sometimes cruise, the motorcycles he would ride into the woods, the car he had to drive to the high school in Kalispell, where he met my mother, the class trip he took in high school to the prison in Deer Lodge, the time he filmed his classmates ice-skating at Woodland Park with a handheld 16 mm camera he loved—I coveted my father's love for his hometown. I understood that my hometown had been sacrificed on a gamble for a future that I wouldn't change for anything, but the gamble had left a small longing, one fulfilled by standing in the light of my father's revelry, and so I moved closer to him as he pointed from the bow at the outcrop of rock a good swim from shore where my father and his friends would sun themselves along with other kids from town whose lives and dreams were lived and dreamed within the tiny town's limits.

•

Staring out at Boston Harbor from the second-floor deck of the parking garage of the University of Massachusetts, I incessantly checked my cell phone as the digital clock ticked toward eight, the scheduled start of my first college teaching job, Intro to Creative Writing, Saturday mornings, from eight to eleven. I'd been relaxing at a friend's house in San Diego when my old friend and Bennington teacher Askold Melnyczuk wrote me in his new capacity as director of the creative writing department at UMass with a job offer; he'd heard I'd moved to Boston and wondered if I was interested in teaching a fiction workshop. I wrote him to say that while the news of my migration was exaggerated—I'd talked about moving to Boston but had no immediate plans to—I'd be happy to accept the position, which had been vacated at the last minute by the original instructor. I cut short my stay in San Diego, flew back to Phoenix to prep for the adventure, and flew to Boston in early September, a few days before the start of my class.

I was well aware that teaching writing at the college level was a much coveted job—if you could teach a couple of classes a semester, it was a nice way to make some change—but I was also dubious about the notion that writing could be taught. The latter didn't give me too much pause, though, since I'd benefited from the writing workshop simply as a venue of encouragement in which I'd been free to develop as a writer, a climate I intended to create in my class at UMass. Too, I'd always been curious about teaching, the satisfaction of making a personal connection and the hope that as a teacher I might inspire someone to write, the way others had inspired me.

I'd been a student in enough fiction workshops not to

be nervous about my first day, though I was nervous about the fact that the class was three hours long. The first day of any class is notoriously short, but I wondered what I could get away with. I'd been briefed by my old Bennington friend Mike, who taught at Emerson College in Boston, that the first day of a once-a-week three-hour class had to be more than handing out the syllabus and going over the course description; he suggested I break the class into groups and assign a writing exercise to be read aloud and workshopped. I found comfort in this advice until I picked up my class roster and saw that only eight people had registered for the early weekend class. The groups could still work with eight, I thought, but only five of the eight showed up, destroying any hope of dividing the class into even-numbered groups.

I welcomed the class, who nodded solemnly, as if graveside. I handed out my syllabus, which was a virtual duplicate of Mike's Emerson syllabus.

I gave the class a chance to look the syllabus over, killing another three minutes. It was barely ten minutes after. I asked if there were any questions; there were none. I'd prepared a lecture on the John Updike story "A&P" almost as an afterthought, grateful that I had. In order to kill some time, I asked the students who had bothered to pick up the anthology beforehand to turn to the story and follow along while I read it out loud. I read deliberately, my voice accompanied by the occasional student shifting in his or her seat. The Updike story killed another twenty minutes or so, and I hoped the student discussion based on the questions I'd prepared would slay another half an hour, making our first class an hour, a third of its scheduled time, but the silence that greeted my first question was a clear indication that the students were only interested in hearing the answers—if they were interested at all—and I provided the answers to my brilliant questions as quickly as I could, handing out a writing assignment and dismissing the class until the following Saturday.

While my inclination was to bolt ahead of the class, I lingered at my desk, needlessly shuffling papers to give students time to ask me questions. A boy who had been lounging in his desk at the back of the room stopped and held out a slip of paper.

"Am I in the right class?" he asked.

I took the paper from him, realizing too late that I'd forgotten Mike's advice about writing the course name on the chalkboard. "The good news is you're in the right classroom," I said. "The bad news is that your class starts in a half an hour." I realized it was bad news for me, too, as I'd just lost a student, though the tide of withdrawals wouldn't stem until the class was down to just four students, who wouldn't be able to generate enough work for three hours' worth of discussion every Saturday even if they each were working on a thousand-page novel.

Another student approached the desk, confiding that English wasn't her first language but that she was hoping my class would help her improve her vocabulary enough to be able to pass the GRE for graduate school.

"That's really not what we do here," I said, balancing my comment so that she wouldn't be discouraged by the class but also wouldn't drop it.

"Well, I like to read, too," she said.

As the paltry class settled into its routine, I quickly began to rely on a certain student to bolster discussion, always disappointed when that student missed class, devastated when she finally dropped halfway through the semester. I came to dread Saturdays, the anxiety visiting me sometime Thursday night as I began preparing my upcoming lecture or poring over the student work, which was often no more than an anecdote stretched into a couple of pages. I put a good face on the class to anyone who asked, though, still appreciative of the opportunity, knowing the circumstances of the Saturday class were an anomaly, a realization that was confirmed when I was hired to teach a creative nonfiction class the following semester at Emerson College.

My Emerson class easily met my expectations about teaching at the collegiate level, and while I believed I was sorely unqualified to teach creative nonfiction, I solicited advice about reading material from practitioners I knew, and endeavored to create a syllabus befitting an advanced class.

A remarkable transformation occurred during my second shot at teaching: I came to learn something about creative nonfiction and fell under the genre's spell, even if the workshop pieces authored by the mostly eighteen-year-old students were largely and sometimes embarrassingly autobiographic, and I loved the challenge of presenting the truth creatively, always counseling my class that while they couldn't make anything up, they could influence their reader by the presentation of details, a skill whose value they'd learn as they got older.

•

That's me at a Books & Brews event at Newtonville Books, the independent bookstore in Boston owned by my friend and landlord Tim Huggins, whom I'd met through Mike. Newtonville Books was Boston's answer to Shakespeare and Company, the great Parisian bookstore owned by expatriate Sylvia Beach that doubled as a meeting place for many prominent writers in the 1920s. Shakespeare and Company had ascended to the pantheon of literary myth, and Newtonville Books seemed destined for similar greatness.

A Southerner by birth, Tim infused his bookstore with small-town touches—for example, Southern Fiction was its own section; you could purchase an Elvis clock like the one on display by asking any one of the employees; and Tim bought the first round at his Books & Brews events, a reading series that traveling authors clamored to be a part of. Tim had agreed to rent the third-floor attic of his house in Watertown to me while I was teaching creative writing, and consequently I attended many Books & Brews events, regardless of whether or not I'd ever heard of the author Tim was hosting. Invariably, these events led to late-night bull sessions on Tim's porch. Over time, a cadre of writers became regulars on Tim's porch, gossiping and gabbing about anything and everything into the early-morning hours. The group was less concerned with replicating the European salons we'd read about in history books than with having a good time and subjecting one another to mild ribbing.

Since I didn't really know anyone in Boston besides Tim and Mike, Newtonville Books became my social lifeline, the readings an appointed good time that I rarely missed. It was on one of these appointments that I happened to be browsing the book table at the front of Tim's store when the girl work-ing behind the counter caught my eye. I gave myself away by doing a double take, which the girl noticed. I introduced myself, and she said her name was Mary.

•

Being with Mary brings a sense of calm absent your life going back as far as you can remember. You surrender completely, allow-ing yourself to be loved, exchanging the ambitions you've held dear for too long for ones that are more personal and satisfying.

•

You're finally able to let go all thoughts of Jenny and the past, realizing how tightly you were holding on to these memo-ries all during your quest to become a famous writer. It isn't a stretch to say that dreams of Jenny following your literary career fueled your desire, much as Gatsby hoped Daisy would wander into one of his parties. But the completeness you feel being with Mary brings clarity, and you admit that you're glad that when Jenny found happiness, she opened herself to its possibilities, as you intend to.

•

You're surprised by how freeing it feels to let go of Jenny and the past, unaware of just how ingrained the narrative became. Fitzgerald blamed the failure of Gatsby partly on Daisy's underdeveloped character. He lamented with hindsight that Daisy was too opaque, that it wasn't clear why Gatsby was convinced she was the love of his life. It is easy to see with hindsight how you craved the TV version of family the Mormons projected, and how Jenny became a symbol of that craving; but even after that illusion faded, the cocoon you spun around those feelings became a hardened cyst just under the skin, a constant hurt you could worry into the present at will. Then a funny thought: You wonder if Jenny is a booklover and if she has even read *The Great Gatsby*, or if she's read it and the narrative meant nothing to her, something you've never considered previously, a measure of how deeply one-sided the entire melodrama was all those years.

•

That's me and Mary posing for pictures at Rosecliff, the Newport, Rhode Island, mansion built by famed architect Stanford White in 1902 for Theresa Fair Oelrichs, heiress to a fortune fueled by the Nevada Comstock silver lode. Not knowing that we would consider renting Rosecliff as the site of our marriage more than a year later, we had made the trip from Boston on the strength of the single fact that some of the party scenes from the Robert Redford version of *The Great Gatsby* had been filmed on the grounds and in the mansion's elegantly adorned ballroom. On a recent road trip across the country, we'd stopped in Saint Paul and stood in front of Fitzgerald's childhood home on Summit Avenue, and on a trip to her parents' house outside of Buffalo she showed me the Lenox Hotel, where Fitzgerald lived when he was a toddler, his father taking a job as a soap salesman for Procter & Gamble. I told her about how I'd stuck my head inside Harry's New York Bar, Fitzgerald's favorite spot in Paris, when I'd stumbled through the city with my brothers the summer before we met. And about how my college friend H—— and I had driven to Fitzgerald's grave in Maryland, a sad final resting place wedged between the clutter of nearby commerce and traffic. Fitzgerald's own funeral had resembled Gatsby's, a rainy day, a scarcity of mourners for someone who had known so many.

Mary and I toured the grounds, admiring the flowers and lawn ornaments, making our way to the back of the palatial estate. As we rounded the house, the great green sloping lawn that ran from the house to the breaker wall came into view, the gray slate of the Atlantic undulating just beyond the wall. We migrated toward the enormous fountain situated near the steps that led from the ballroom and out under a pink-and-white-striped canopy. I reminded Mary about the fountain in the film version of Gatsby, speculating that the filmmakers must've laid down a wooden floor to accommodate the outdoor dancing, then taken it up again before firing up the rain machine that unleashed the torrent that sent the principal actors and extras alike running for cover. My thoughts drifted as we strolled down the lawn toward the ocean. I wondered what Fitzgerald would've thought of the film of his best book.

I wondered what he would've thought about the fact that the book had even been adapted, knowing that he'd died in near poverty, his books collecting dust in his publisher's warehouse, the once-famous writer forgotten in his own lifetime, a sad and cruel reward for so much effort and ambition.

We congregated with a few other visitors at the breaker wall. The weather was turning, the sun displaced from its domain by cloud cover that would later issue a light rain. I peered over the breaker wall at the walkway that was no doubt the handiwork of the Preservation Society of Newport County, and Mary said that you could in fact take a walking tour of the various mansions by following the sidewalk as it wound along the coastline. A blackness caught my eye as I stared out at the ocean, the word detest spray-painted on the outside of the breaker wall, which called to mind the profanity scrawled on the front steps of Gatsby's house after he'd died, and, as in the book, I imagined the handiwork to be that of a local kid, maybe from neighboring Middletown or an equally middle-class town with proximity to Newport, sick of the tourists who flocked annually along the Cliff Walk, speeding through his or her town without so much as a glance, intently focused on the gem that lay at the tip of the peninsula. Then I imagined the scrawl having been written by any one of the houses' previous owners, a cry of self-revulsion about what it took to become lord of a manor like Rosecliff, the self-sacrifice and body count souring the owner's breath, the gleaming white terra-cotta mansion burning out his eyes as he stalked from room to room, coloring the breathtaking view of the Atlantic Ocean from the breaker wall, so that instead of wondering at the horizon, the owner stared bitterly at the gray water, choking back rafts of wasted time and energy as they rolled in with the tide.

As we strolled back toward the house to take more pictures before the imminent rain, I noticed a small boy running around the fountain. The boy bore a striking resemblance to me in my youth—the same blond hair shaped by a bowl cut, the same restless energy that wore down everyone around him. The boy's father disappeared under the pink-and-white canopy to press his face against the window, then reemerged to take a picture of the ocean from the back steps.

"Where'd you go?" the boy asked as he circled the fountain.

The question lingered and I wondered what the seven-year-old me would've thought if he'd known all that lay ahead. The sole piece of useful advice he could've used is this: Life is not a romantic proposition, and the inability to acknowledge that simple fact and, worse, the desperate scheming to make life conform to a personal romantic vision are useless folly, and the cost is always a broken heart.

And yet.

CPSIA information can be obtained
at www.ICGtesting.com
Printed in the USA
LVOW12s0147180317
527664LV00003B/3/P